Fill the House with Quilting

Eileen Westfall

Sterling Publishing Co., Inc.   New York

Designed by Judy Morgan

Edited by Jeanette Green

Computer Graphics by Nancy Rowland of Sound Images, Inc.

Photographs by Shel Izen

Library of Congress Cataloging-in-Publication Data

Westfall, Eileen.
   Fill the house with quilting / by Eileen Westfall.
         p.   cm.
   Includes index.
   ISBN 0-8069-8754-5
      1. Appliqué—Patterns.   2. Patchwork—Patterns.   I. Title.
TT779.W47   1993
746.46—dc20   92-41348
                                                                   CIP

                2   4   6   8   10   9   7   5   3

First paperback edition published in 1994 by
Sterling Publishing Company, Inc.
387 Park Avenue South, New York, N.Y. 10016
© 1993 by Eileen Westfall
Distributed in Canada by Sterling Publishing
℅ Canadian Manda Group, P.O. Box 920, Station U
Toronto, Ontario, Canada M8Z 5P9
Distributed in Great Britain and Europe by Cassell PLC
Villiers House, 41/47 Strand, London WC2N 5JE, England
Distributed in Australia by Capricorn Link Ltd.
P.O. Box 665, Lane Cove, NSW 2066
Printed in Hong Kong
All rights reserved

Sterling ISBN 0-8069-8754-5 Trade
            0-8069-8755-3 Paper

CONTENTS

ACKNOWLEDGMENTS

I wish to thank many people for their help with this book—John Mansfield for set painting; Sue Osoteo of Edmonds Flower Shop for fresh flowers; Sue von Jentzen for making the quilts Heart-and-Tulip stringer, Hearts-and-Flowers wall hanging, and "Tell Me, My Heart, If This Be Love"; Jana Baldridge Vargas for making the Log Cabin tablecloth and Log Cabin pillow; Marta Estes for making the Nine-Patch in a Nine-Patch Quilt and Shaded Evergreens Quilt. Also much thanks to Shel Izen for photographing these quilt projects and to Nancy Rowland for graphics.

INTRODUCTION

I f you've developed a keen interest in the exciting art of quilting, you know how addicting it can be. First, you begin making a small project, next a little larger one, and finally a full-size quilt. Then you begin accumulating assorted quilts and quilted things.

That's the way it was with me when I became addicted to patchwork, appliqué, and quilting! From the first patchwork I made (a pillow, by hand), my love for quilting grew so much that I wanted to be surrounded by quilts in my home. I wanted to adorn everything with quilted beauty.

As I got caught up studying different designs and projects, the idea of using my projects for interior decorating seemed the ideal thing to do. I began making these quilt projects the central theme of my house. I am glad that quilts naturally blend with the antiques and country styles I've chosen for my home.

I have been designing, stitching, and collecting for about twenty years. My house is decorated and filled with quilting. I've covered my walls with many antique quilts as well as those of my own design.

I have enjoyed designing the projects in these pages and hope you, too, will want to fill your house with quilting. I've included thirty projects for your kitchen, entry hall, children's room, living and family rooms, and for holiday celebrations. I hope you delight in making them. May you have hours of pleasure.

Eileen Westfall

QUILTING BASICS

Appliqué

Appliqué is the method of attaching one fabric shape over another for a specific desired result. Usually, the fabric being appliquéd is a color while the fabric being appliquéd on is a light or creamy background, to provide contrast.

Baltimore Album quilts are created from appliqué as are Hawaiian quilts. Quilts may be completely appliquéd on a large single piece of fabric with no patchwork at all. Quilts can have appliqué on each block. Sewing the blocks together makes it a patchwork and so the quilt is both patchwork and appliqué.

There are many different methods of appliqué, although the basic distinctions are between machine and hand appliqué. Projects in this book featuring appliqué have been made by hand; however, it is possible to use a machine appliqué method for the designs.

Machine Appliqué

In my early years, I used machine appliqué for designs since it was quick and easy. I had thought hand appliqué was too tedious to attempt. The chief advantage of machine appliqué is its speed. The drawbacks are that unless you have a machine that does great zigzag work, it can be frustrating. Some machines balk when performing a close zigzag satin-stitch, and you can end up with a big knot of thread or simply tear your fabric. It is easier for machine appliqué to fray in the washing machine, and the finished product is hard to repair. Machine appliqué gives the product a more modern look, while hand appliqué make things look more traditional.

Machine Appliqué Method

First, cut out the item to be appliquéd, *without* seam allowance. Glue the fabric shape to the background fabric, carefully placing it in the spot desired. Press the two to secure. Cut out a piece of tear-away Pellon slightly larger than the shape to be appliquéd. The Pellon will stabilize the item you plan to appliqué. Pin the Pellon to the back side of the background fabric, lining it up with the shape to be appliquéd.

Set your sewing machine on a fine satin-stitch, and experiment with the tension on a sample piece of fabric. Test the stitching flow, making sure the fabric does not bunch up. Use more stitches per inch if your fabric bunches. By machine, sew around the edges of the fabric being appliquéd. Be sure to catch the entire edge of the shape in the satin-stitch so that it will be strong and will not fray.

After you finish your appliqué, remove the Pellon from the back side.

Hand Appliqué

Many interesting methods of hand appliqué can make it a delight rather than a tedious chore. Through my years of quilting, I have come to prefer the look of the hand-appliquéd works. Though it takes more time than by machine, I think the results are worth it. Hand appliqué more closely represents the methods of quilt makers through the centuries. It produces a more classic look. Here is my preferred method of hand appliqué, using paper.

Hand Appliqué Method

Photocopy two copies of the pattern to be appliquéd. From one copy, cut out the shape in the fabric desired. From the second copy, trim away the seam allowance, cutting on the broken (stitching) line, thereby creating a template for the appliqué.

Center the paper template on the fabric shape and fold the seam allowances towards the back side of the paper. By hand, baste around the shape with contrasting thread. Be sure the fabric is right side out.

After you baste the fabric shape to the paper shape, press it with a hot steam iron. Remove the basting thread and the paper shape from the fabric shape.

Glue the back side of the pressed fabric shape with a glue stick, and set it on the background fabric, making it ready for appliqué. Sew the glued shape to the background by hand, using small stitches. Try to hide stitches by bringing the needle underneath the fabric shape.

Basic Supplies

Despite the old saying "It's a poor workman who blames his tools," I believe that to do good quilt work, you need to have the right tools. When you have all the right supplies, you will be able to create your quilt more easily, and you'll be less frustrated. Below are some basic supplies and information you'll need to work with the projects in this book.

Fabric

Use only 100 percent cotton fabric when making these projects. Polyester or polyester blends pucker and pull, and they do not produce the fine results that all-cotton fabric does.

If you are not sure your fabric is 100 percent cotton, test it by pulling a few threads from the fabric, lighting a match, and holding the threads over the flame. Polyester or synthetic Fiberfil will produce black smoke and have the faint smell of plastic. You can also test the fabric by ironing. Cotton fabrics will crease more easily than polyester or synthetics.

Fabric amounts given in these pages are based on 45-inch-wide fabrics.

Always prewash your fabrics. This will eliminate any shrinking early, rather than later, after your project is completed. To remind yourself which fabric in your collection has been washed, label the washed fabric with a bright sticker in one corner.

Glue Stick

Several projects require a glue stick. Be sure the one you use specifically states that it is for fabric use.

Manila Envelope

After you have used a pattern, you will want to save the pieces for possible reuse. You could keep them in a large manila envelope. If you like, you could tape or glue the envelope inside the back cover of this book to keep everything together.

Marking Pens

I have a collection of antique quilts. A few of them bear the sad remnants of poor marking methods from yesteryear—done with gray pencil! I think this ruins the look of the quilt, but in those days, quilters did not have the luxury of erasable marking pens.

Though there are many brands of erasable marking pens, they usually come in two forms—one with fading ink and one you can wash out with water. Each has its pros and cons. The fading ink is light and usually fades before you have completed your work. This can be irritating since you may have to go back and re-mark the fabric. I use this kind of marking pen on small projects that can be completed quickly. The marking pen that washes out with water usually has a very bright color. After you wash it out, you'll often find that when dry, traces of the pen reappear, so you'll have to wet the project again. Sometimes you'll need to re-wet the fabric many times to finally get the marks out.

I cannot recommend the marking pencils in today's market. Most do not provide removal instructions. Someone who quilted a sample for one of my books used a yellow marking pencil. She called me in a panic and said she had completed the quilt but could not get the yellow marks out. I worked on the piece, scrubbing it with a stain remover prewash stick (risking losing the desired fabric colors). After scrubbing and soaking many hours, the pencil faded enough to take a photo of the sample. However, the wall hanging still bears the telltale yellow pencil marks when seen live.

Experiment with marking pens to prevent yourself from making an indelible mistake.

Needles

Quilting needles are required; I prefer sizes 8, 10, or 12. They are usually called "betweens" on the package. The smaller the needle, the easier it is to make a small stitch.

Pins

Be sure to get the best pins available, even if they are more expensive. Dull pins are hard to work with; they can snag and pull fabric.

Quilting Tape

Quilting tape is actually paper tape (also known as *masking tape*) and is available at hardware stores as well as quilting shops. It comes in widths from 1/64 inch to 1 inch. It will really help you in the quilting process, giving the quilt a more professional look.

Sandpaper

A great trick to aid cutting fabric is to glue a piece of sandpaper to the back of a pattern with the rough side out. (Be sure to cut out sandpaper with old, dull shears!) The sandpaper will help weigh down the pattern, and grip the fabric, allowing you to cut more accurately. Remember that accuracy is the key to professional-looking patchwork.

Scissors

Be sure you have a good pair of sharp scissors so that cutting will go smoothly and you won't be fighting the fabric. If you have a good pair that has become dull, it's worthwhile to get them sharpened. Be sure to have scissors at your house for fabric use only. Keep other pairs exclusively for cutting paper and for other things.

Seam Allowances

Most seam allowances in this book are 1/4 inch. A few of the projects do have certain small detail parts that use 1/8-inch seams. When this is the case, the smaller seam allowance will be clearly labelled beside the pattern piece in question.

Seam Ripper

If you make a mistake and need to remake a seam, a seam ripper sure beats taking out those stitches with a pin.

Don't get discouraged when you make a mistake. Anything worth making is worth making right. Since quilting is very exacting, mistakes are bound to happen. Some things look better the second time around.

Sewing Machine

Every project in this book requires some use of the sewing machine. Make sure your sewing machine is in good working order and has been oiled recently. Start each project with a new needle. Also be sure the needle you use is the correct weight for cotton fabrics.

I own an inexpensive basic sewing machine that does straight seams and zigzag. My machine doesn't have a computer brain, nor does it stitch fifty decorative stitches. It cost around $160. It's a great machine and does all the things I need for any quilting procedure.

Thread

Use coordinating thread when sewing. When young, I made a yellow patchwork quilt and used navy blue thread to sew it together! I was out of white or yellow thread, and I wasn't aware of my mistake. The blue showed through and made the patchwork look dingy.

Use only 100 percent cotton thread when sewing these projects together. Polyester thread will pull and pucker.

When quilting, use only quilting thread. Since quilting thread is treated with wax, it is coarser than regular thread. The coarseness of the quilting thread helps the stitches stand out and also strengthens the finished work.

Thimble

I have a confession to make: in my many years of sewing, I've never been comfortable using a thimble. I am left-handed; so I do many things backwards and upside down. This could be the source of my "thimble block." I've used every kind of thimble made—yes, even the soft, leather ones. My fingers remain cut and bleeding when I do a large quilt project.

I don't recommend this to anyone! I urge you to use a thimble for quilting. It protects your fingers, pushes the needle through the fabric easily, and you'll enjoy painless quilting.

Photocopying

When you decide to make a particular pattern in this book, photocopy the pattern; that way, you'll keep the book intact. Be sure to find a good copy outlet, since cheap photocopy machines distort lines and make the pattern inaccurate.

Sewing Binding to the Quilt

Pin the binding around the entire edge of the quilt or wall hanging front. Turn the ends under, away from the right side of the quilt, and pin them in place. Stitch the binding to the quilt ¼ inch from the edge.

After you complete the stitching, take out the pins, and turn the binding to the back of the quilt. Turn the binding under ¼ inch, and pin along the seam line created when the binding was sewn to the front of the quilt. Pin it in place.

By hand, stitch the binding to the quilt back, using small stitches so they won't show. Be sure your stitches are about ¼ inch apart. To be sure that hemming stitches don't appear on the front of the quilt, catch the seam allowance rather than going through the entire quilt. Remove pins.

Cutting and Sewing Bias Binding

1. Trim selvage edges from both sides of a square of fabric.

2. Mark the bias center line by drawing a line from one corner to the opposite corner.

3. Mark 1¾-inch-wide strips under and over the center bias line.

4. Cut the strips along the marked lines.

5. Stitch the strip ends together as shown below.

6. Press seams open.

7. Trim off the seam allowances that hang over the sides of the bias strips.

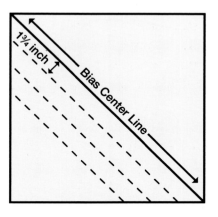

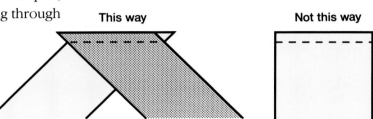

This way **Not this way**

Color

For these quilt projects, color is as important as design. Each person has his or her own favorite colors—colors he or she naturally gravitates towards. Color has a strong influence on whether or not a quilt appeals to you. You will probably want to make some projects in colors that go with your own home.

I joke with my quilting group about being the only person in the group whose favorite color isn't blue! Since I'm a "spring" (according to seasonal color analysts), I love greens, peaches, and purples. My friends think I am kind of strange since I don't fill my house with blue. I had to remind myself when choosing colors for the quilt projects in this book that people have different color preferences. I tried to use a wide range of colors—warm and cool—in the quilt samples shown in these pages to be certain that various preferences are represented.

Color Wheel

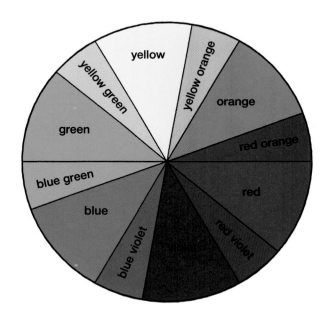

Color Basics

Here are some color basics. The three *primary colors* are red, yellow, and blue; all other colors are derived from these three. *Secondary colors* are green, orange, purple. *Tertiary colors* are red violet, red orange, yellow orange, yellow green, blue green, and blue violet. *Neutral tones*—white, black, grey, and beige—are not considered colors. A *tint* of a color means white has been added; a *shade* means black has been added.

There are three basic color schemes. *Monochromatic* colors include shades (color + black added) or tints (color + white added) of the same color. *Analogous* or related colors lie next to each other on the color wheel. *Complementary* colors are opposite each other on the color wheel.

When I am not sure what color will go with a certain patchwork pattern, I experiment before cutting all the pieces. I often make a mock-up of the patchwork block. I begin with graph paper and draw the actual size of the quilt block, as well as the patchwork design. Then I start playing with the colors and fabric I may want to use in the block. Then, I ask myself what the dominant (D), secondary (S), and background (B) pieces in the block are. I mark them with *D*, *S*, or *B*, accordingly.

For best results, I usually choose a dark fabric for the dominant blocks, a medium color for secondary, and a light color or neutral for the background blocks.

You can also be successful by using the same formula in reverse, with a dark background, medium secondary, and light dominant design in your quilt block. I have seen this color scheme in many Amish quilts.

After I have chosen fabrics that might work on the block, I cut out the shapes, without seam allowances, and glue them in the appropriate positions on the patchwork design. That way, I have a sample of the proposed quilt in living color. And you'll be able to experiment with possible color combinations without cutting all the pieces out and sewing them together, slowly realizing that the combination is *not* pleasing. But don't get tied to a formula; you can successfully experiment. Have fun with color—the combinations are limitless. Just let loose your imagination!

Embroidery Stitches

Back Stitch

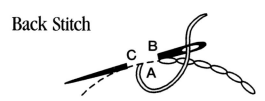

Bring the needle through the fabric from back to front. Reenter about ⅛ inch to the right and, at the same time, bring the needle tip out ⅛ inch to the left of your original entry. For the next stitch, bring the needle back to the center point and out ⅛ inch to the left of the needle's first exit point. Repeat, forming a smooth outline stitch.

French Knot

First, bring the needle up at A. Wrap the thread around the needle two or three times.

Then, insert the needle close to where the thread first emerged.

Draw the thread snugly around the needle and push the needle through.

The finished knot.

Satin Stitch

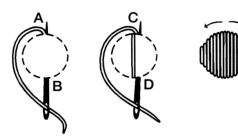

Bring the needle through at the center top of the area to be satin-stitched. Reenter at the backside of the fabric at the center bottom of the area—nose, eye, or other solid stitched design.

Continue this process, bringing each new stitch out from the top of the area as close to the last stitch as possible.

Work left to right to the side edge of the center area of stitching. Then come back to the center point, and work right to the left to the other side edge of the area.

Chain Stitch

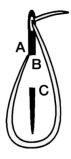

Bring the thread through from the back to the front of the fabric.

Insert the needle back through the fabric close to where the thread last came up.

Bring the needle up a short distance away, keeping the working thread under the needle's tip. Draw out the needle over the loop.

Repeat this process to form a chain.

Fabric Selection

Fabric selection is a personal matter. So, I'll simply suggest guidelines and talk about storage.

Here Are Some Ideas

I never buy fabric just to have fabric on hand. When I enter a fabric store, I usually go straight to the 100 percent cotton section. Then, I scan the aisles to take a superficial look at all the fabrics I see. Then, I concentrate on color and design. If I get excited about a certain fabric, even though I may not have a specific project in mind, I know that sometime down the road the fabric will be great in *something*. When I feel this way, I know the fabric will not end up collecting dust on the shelf or have to be given away.

What makes a fabric beautiful and just right for my purposes? Lots of elements go into wonderful fabric design, but here are a few questions to ask yourself when you're not sure whether you should choose a given fabric.

Are the colors right for the use you have in mind?

How often have you seen a print you like but wish it were in another color? A friend showed me 3 yards of a great print in a color that we both knew she wouldn't be able to live with. She loved the design, but the color would stop her from ever using it. So, she lost the money she spent and also had a sick feeling about what might have been. Even if you are crazy about the print in question, don't get it unless you also feel that way about the color.

Do the colors blend with other fabric colors selected for the project?

I usually choose a main fabric for a quilt pattern, and then begin the process of selecting "supporting players." I take a swatch of the main print to the fabric store, so that I can be sure about the color, print compatibility, and more. Unless these supporting prints are as perfect as the main fabric, your project won't turn out as nice as it could.

Are the flowers, plaids, or stripes a good design? What do you like about the design? What style or feeling does the fabric design bring to mind?

Personally, I look for flowers, butterflies, or any realistic motif. I don't like abstract things. Though I respect the contemporary quilter, that just isn't *my* style. I love delicate small prints—flowers or buds with small vines and ferns wrapping all around. Large, splashy prints in patchwork—like chintz prints with large flowers—offer too much competition with the patchwork design. I think they should be reserved for large patchwork patterns. I think the smaller prints more closely resemble the original fabric prints used on the prairie when the early American quilters were selecting fabric. I want my print to have that traditional feeling. A few modern fabric designers have accomplished this.

When looking at fabric, I consider what essence it suggests. If the fabric feels or looks like a dime-store print—old, faded, and poorly designed—it usually doesn't excite me. But if it seems elegant, delicate, or romantic, the fabric usually draws my attention!

When you are choosing fabric, allow yourself time to answer these questions. If you savor your final fabric choices, won't have to give fabrics away.

Fabric Storage

I store my fabric in a closet on shelves. If you don't have an available closet, try a bookcase with deep shelves. It really helps to keep your fabric all in one place so that you'll know exactly what you have.

I also recommend that you stack your neatly folded fabric according to color. You could then place complementary colors next to each other. That way, when you want a print in a particular color, you can just take out your stack of that color and check your inventory for just the right print. This is easier than rummaging through bags of wadded-up fabric.

This also helps you keep track of how much fabric you have of a particular print. Many people see a piece of fabric they like and buy several yards. I suggest keeping a tag on the end of each large piece of fabric with the total yards. Each time you use the fabric, simply adjust the amount on the tag.

Having your fabric in order can give you a good feeling. Often when you're working on a project, things can get pretty messed up. Each time you begin a new project, take a couple hours to straighten your fabric closet. Once you're organized, you'll feel more ready to start the next project.

How you store fabric can influence your creativity since fabric is a basic quilting tool. It deserves attention and care. You'll enjoy it all the more.

Patchwork

Patchwork involves actually piecing and stitching pieces of fabric together to form a specific design. The projects in this book have detailed assembly diagrams to guide you. Here are some helpful tips for successful patchwork.

Cutting Fabric Pieces

Accuracy is most important when creating a patchwork, and cutting out fabric pattern pieces is at the heart of that accuracy. So, take extra care when cutting. Using sandpaper on the back of pattern pieces helps (see p. 8). If you don't use the sandpaper method, be sure to pin the pattern close to the edge of the cloth since this will help to ensure that you'll cut the fabric to the precise pattern shape.

Rotary cutters have revolutionized cutting out patchwork. They provide the most accurate way to cut blocks and strips. I recommend rotary cutters, but advise that you take a class to learn how to use them. If you try to teach yourself, you could ruin fabric or cut yourself. If you aren't familiar with rotary cutters, stop into your local fabric or quilt shop and ask.

Before cutting, *press the fabric* with a hot steam iron. This will prevent any wrinkles or folds that could alter the final shape.

Cut fabric on the bias. Set each pattern on the fabric's lengthwise *or* crosswise grain, unless directed otherwise in pattern. Pieces cut on the fabric's bias will have extra elasticity and may not fit other patchwork pieces.

Finished sizes for projects indicate measurements the projects should be if your piecing and everything turns out perfectly. It is often difficult to be accurate. Rather than cutting out a back or Fiberfil shape in the measurements given, use your patchwork front shape as a pattern; that way, your back and Fiberfil will always fit perfectly. If, however, you are crackerjack at cutting and sewing patchwork, you can cut out the exact sizes for the backing or padding given.

Sewing Fabric Pieces

Set your machine to a short stitch length. Long, loose stitches can come undone, and a small, close stitch will strengthen the patchwork.

Back tack a few stitches at the end of each seam. Since seams often come unravelled at the ends, back tacking will prevent this.

Check and maintain seam allowances for each pattern. Most seam allowances in this book are ¼ inch, unless otherwise noted. Any variation from the uniform seam allowances will throw off the patchwork. Seams will not meet as they should, and the project's shape will be distorted. You could attach a piece of tape on your sewing machine ¼ inch away from the needle to guide you so that you won't veer away from a uniform ¼-inch seam allowance.

Baste seams with thread or pins to ensure exactness.

Fold seam allowances towards darker colors when sewing rows together, patching a block, or sewing blocks together. Press them in place. Lighter colors are generally used for the background and are most likely to be quilted. Folding seam allowances away from the area to be quilted means that you won't have to push your quilting needle through bulky seam allowances.

Piping Ends

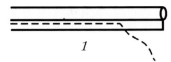

1

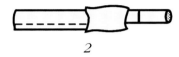

2

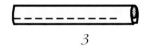

3

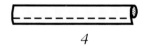

4

5

1. Measure the length of the piping needed and add ½ inch. Remove 1 inch of stitching. Pull back the piping cover.

2. Trim the piping to the exact length you'll need.

3. Fold the piping cover fabric under so that it lines up exactly with the piping end.

4. Restitch the area where stitching was removed.

5. Prepare each piping end using this method so that ends will be smooth when they meet. Tack the ends together on the underside so that the stitching won't show.

Quilting

Quilting consists of short running stitches, usually through two layers of fabric and one of padding. Many people believe that any tied coverlets may be classified as quilts as long as they include patchwork. This isn't true; tied quilts are actually comforters. Only quilts with running stitches binding the three layers together qualify as quilts.

In this book, some projects are quilted with only two layers (a quilt top and Fiberfil) so that you can easily make them three-dimensional by stuffing them. All projects here are quilted by hand. Many projects require *single outline quilting*; others require *motif quilting*. Whenever possible, quilt the lightest color patches; that will allow darker color patches to be displayed more prominently.

Quilting Methods

Here are some definitions and tips about quilting appliqué designs.

Single Outline Quilting follows the seam line of a given pattern, stitching ¼ inch away from the seam.

Double Outline Quilting is done on both sides on the seam, ¼ inch from the seam, following the seam line.

Motif Quilting involves quilting a specific design in an unpatched area, such as a border or in the enter of a block.

Diagonal Quilting is done on the diagonal that runs *through* the patchwork design rather than around it.

Quilting in the Ditch involves quilting right on the seam itself, following the line of the patchwork.

Single Outline Quilting

Double Outline Quilting

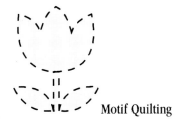

Motif Quilting

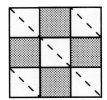

Diagonal Quilting

Tips on Quilting

Use tiny stitches. A goal to work towards is between 8 and 12 stitches per inch.

Hide your knot. When quilting through three layers, pull your first stitch through the project from back to front. Then, give an extra tug to make the knot go through the back fabric but not the padding and the upper fabric. Your knot is now hidden, and the back quilting remains as attractive as the front.

Be sure to baste. For large projects basting is a necessity, but for small projects, basting is not always needed. Basting does help stabilize fabric, and it assures that there will be no bunching during quilting. Consult the basting section (p. 17) for details.

Use a quilting hoop—heavier than an embroidery hoop—to control the fabric while quilting. The hoop may come with a stand attached. If you quilt projects with a hoop, they'll be more portable.

Or, use a quilting frame. A quilting frame is usually a wooden rectangle the full size of an actual quilt. Traditional quilters of past ages often used a frame. They pinned the quilt to the frame and stabilized it along the sides every few inches. Then groups could work from a frame set up in a large room, such as a basement. Today most quilters find quilting frames too large for their homes; so, they prefer the hoop.

Preparing the Batting

Batting comes in two basic forms—one-piece pre-sized batting usually folded into a roll in a plastic bag, and batting by the yard that comes on a roll and can be cut to the desired length. Batting on a roll is almost always 60 inches wide. Batting by the yard can be less expensive, but you do need to sew it together to create a width that accommodates your quilt top. For these projects, I recommend that you use the lightest-weight batting possible. Batting comes in varying weights, but I prefer not to struggle with a heavy batting. Quilting goes much faster, and it is more enjoyable with lightweight batting.

Joining Batting

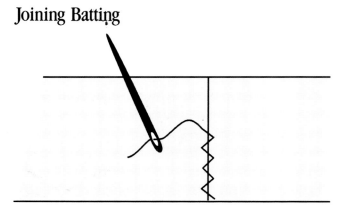

If you decide to use the batting on the roll, you'll need to sew it together to create the necessary width.

Decide the length of batting needed and cut two lengths. Set the lengths side by side on a clean surface, such as the floor. Using a zigzag stitch with needle and thread, sew the lengths together, as shown below. Do *not* allow Fiberfil edges to overlap. Set the quilt top on the sewn batting, and trim the batting to the same size as the top.

Marking in Preparation for Embroidery or Quilting

Marking is important in quilting since it is the blueprint for the actual procedure. If not done accurately, it can affect the appearance of the finished quilt. Marking is not easy, since fabric can move around, changing the exactness of the design. You need to concentrate when marking.

A light box, often used by photographers, is a great marking tool. A plastic light box, usually 10×12 inches, houses a low-watt bulb. This handy tool costs about $75.

If you don't want to invest in a light box, here are two other ways to mark cloth.

Window Method for Marking Small Pieces

Tape the design template you plan to copy to a window with lots of sun coming through.

Tape the fabric over the template, carefully placing it exactly where you want the design.

Trace the quilt design or embroidery motif with an erasable quilt-marking pen.

Lamp Method for Marking Large Pieces

You'll need a lamp with a large circle opening at the top of the shade.

Set a pane of glass on top of the lampshade with the lamp turned on. (You could take a pane of glass out of a large picture frame.)

Tape the pattern to be transferred to the glass.

Set the quilt top over the lamp, aligning the top to the exact spot you plan to mark.

Trace the design with a quilt-marking pen.

Adjust the top as needed to completely mark the fabric.

Preparing the Quilt Back

Since most fabrics are only 45 inches wide, that means quilt backs have to be pieced. I have seen many creative quilt backs, including double-sided quilts with a quilt on both the back and front. I have seen quilts with a few blocks sewn decoratively on the back. Below is a simple way of preparing a quilt back. Use your own imagination and creativity to embellish it.

Quilt Back

Cut the fabric length allotted for your specific project in half, making two equal pieces. Trim off one of the selvage edges on each piece of fabric.

Set the fabric pieces, with right sides together, lining up the trimmed selvage edges exactly. Sew the lengths back together. Open the sewn back, and press the seams open to prevent extra bulk in the center of the quilt.

Lay the quilt back down on a smooth, flat surface (I use the floor), *wrong* side up.

To back the quilt, set a Fiberfil piece centered as accurately as possible.

Now set the quilt top on the Fiberfil, lined up exactly.

Trim the quilt back, allowing 2 inches extra on each side since backs sometimes shrink a little in the quilting process.

Basting the Quilt

Basting is not a fun part of the quilt-making process, to my way of thinking, but it is important. Without basting, your lovely quilt top that was so carefully made can appear hopelessly bunched up and ruin the finished quilt.

I have a wall hanging buried deep in an old trunk that I don't like to think about. It is a basket design I worked on long and hard. I was in a hurry, wanting to quilt everything as soon as I completed the top.

I did a sloppy job basting, so, after I quilted a few blocks I began to see puckers and small twists. I told myself that after it was all quilted, it would look fine. But the more I quilted, the more I knew I had cheated myself on the basting and was paying the price.

After about four blocks and a few feather-stitch designs on the border, I packed the wall hanging away sadly. I promised myself that someday I would tear the basting threads out, baste properly and start over. So far, I haven't gotten around to it. The moral is to take the time to baste your quilt properly the first time—it's worth it.

Think of quilting like dessert, the special treat after the long patchwork or appliqué process! If something looks great in patchwork, it will look even better when quilted.

Here are some tips on making the basting process less boring.

Listen to music as you baste.

Baste with a friend, conversing as you work.

Break basting times down into 15-minute sections; do another chore or take a breath of fresh air to break the monotony between sections.

Promise yourself a small reward for doing a good job of basting.

Basting involves just using long running stitches to secure the top, batting, and back of the quilt together. I usually baste on the floor. I first thread many needles with bright contrasting thread in lengths about three or four feet long. Once I place the quilt elements together smoothly, I begin to baste a row about 4 inches into the top end of the quilt, working from side to side. As I baste, working down the body of the quilt, I start to roll the already basted part—carefully to avoid any bunching. When the horizontal basting has been done, I then repeat the process vertically.

One of the joys of basting is that when you finally complete the quilting, you can remove it. I'm tickled to see my finished quilting stitches uncomplicated by basting!

ENTRYWAYS

*M*any *interior designers consider the house entryway the most important area of the house. I agree, since it's on the threshold that we gain our first impressions. It's fun to set a mood in the entry hall that reflects the theme of your home. So, to truly fill the house with quilting, you need to start with your entryway—whether it's a simple front door, hallway, foyer, or entire room.*

What kind of entryway do you have? Whether your space is large or small, you can decorate with quilting. Why not dream up original ways to add zest to your entry? Start by making quilted articles to decorate whatever space you have.

The Heart-and-Tulip *stringer includes patchwork tulips and heart shapes sewn together end-to-end to form a broad band or string. You could display this piece on your front door—inside or outside. You can add more patchwork hearts to the stringer as you wish, to suit the size of the area you want to decorate.*

The Rainbow Welcome *wreath, made in many colors, will harmonize with most color schemes. Edged with prairie points, the wreath has lots of multicolored ribbons. Your Rainbow Welcome wreath could be hung on a wall that faces the door to greet visitors.*

"Enter with a Peaceful Heart," a wall hanging in the shape of a semicircle, features a dove in the center. This wall hanging suggests warmth and friendliness and can be displayed in a prominent spot in your entryway.

The "Loving Friends Are Welcome Here" wall hanging features a heart-adorned gate and an arbor with little flowers peeking over the fence. You can hang this gem on a wall surrounded by your favorite decorations.

The Stars-and-Stripes *mail basket cover in bold red, white, and blue is designed to hold the day's mail. You can set this decorated basket on a table or chair in your entryway.*

These quilted projects work well with other country or traditional decorations, such as dried flower bouquets, wreaths, painted wood plaques, or pictures.

The projects in this chapter are constructed in an assortment of colors. You can make them in your favorite interior decorating colors and see how well they work in your entryway. You can make most of these quilts in a day—so you'll quickly create an entryway with pleasing quilted things.

"ENTER WITH A PEACEFUL HEART" SIGN

Supplies

½ yard cranberry fabric for back, D strips, and heart

⅛ yard white fabric for dove

skein of 6-strand embroidery thread in cranberry, navy blue, green, grey, black, blue (You'll need a full skein in *navy blue* only; for all other colors, just small amounts are necessary.)

¼ yard light blue-and-white print for A main block

1 yard of white single-fold bias tape for binding edges

⅓ yard of lightweight Fiberfil

quilting needle

quilting thread

erasable quilt marker

small embroidery hoop

lightweight bracket for hanging

Directions

Finished size: 9½ × 16½ inches

Trace the A shape on the light blue fabric, and then trace the words "ENTER WITH A PEACEFUL HEART" along the edge as shown on the pattern. Also trace the dove shape centered on A as shown in the pattern. This will help as a guideline later when appliquéing the dove. Next, trace leaves, vines, and berries using the pattern as a guide. Embroider the words, leaves, and vines using a small hoop. Use a *back stitch* for words and vines, *French knots* for the berries, and a *satin stitch* for the leaves and dots between words. Use three strands of embroidery thread.

Now trace the dove shape on white fabric. At the designated spot on the dove, trace the bird's eye. With *one* strand of black embroidery thread for the eye, use the *back stitch* to outline the eye and lashes. Fill in the eye shape with two strands of thread using the *satin stitch*.

Next, cut out the embroidered A semicircle shape. Cut out the embroidered dove shape. Trace the wing feather lines. Appliqué the dove on the marked spot on A. Trace the beak on the dove as shown in the diagram. Outline the beak with the *back stitch* using *one* strand; fill it in with the *satin stitch* using two strands.

Appliqué the heart to the dove, following the placement line on the pattern. Next, sew the D–2 strip to the bottom and the D–1 strip to the curved edge as shown below. Use the sign as a pattern, and cut out both a back and Fiberfil shape. Put the back, Fiberfil, and top together, and baste them in preparation for quilting.

For the quilt wall hanging, quilt around the dove, leaves, vines, outer edge of A, and two rows of quilting around D–1 and D–2. Also, quilt the wing bottom edges as traced. Bind the outside edges of the sign with bias tape. Attach a bracket to the top center edge of the sign.

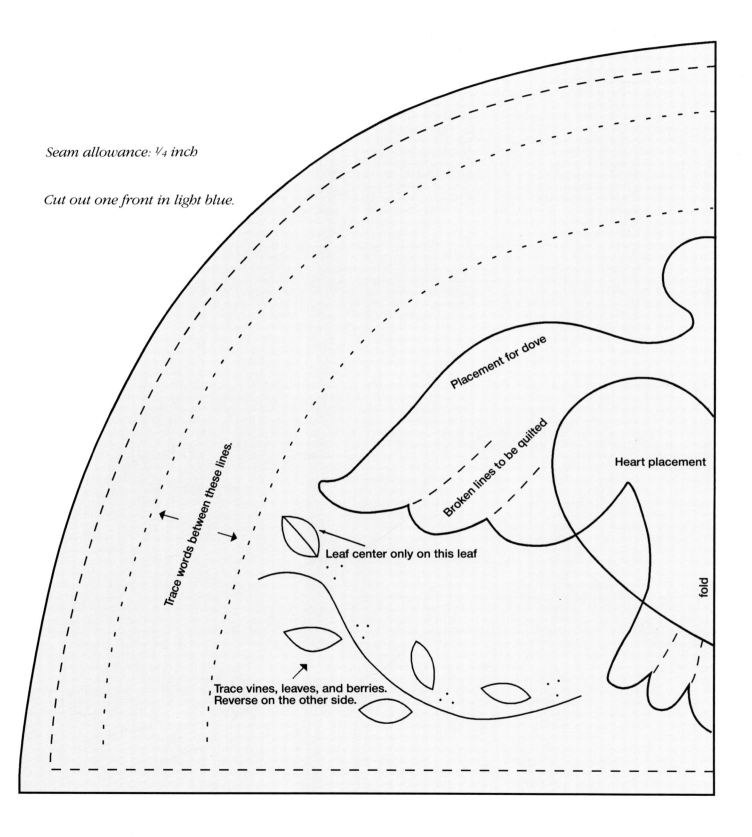

Seam allowance: ¼ inch

Cut out one front in light blue.

Placement for dove

Broken lines to be quilted

Heart placement

Trace words between these lines.

Leaf center only on this leaf

Trace vines, leaves, and berries.
Reverse on the other side.

fold

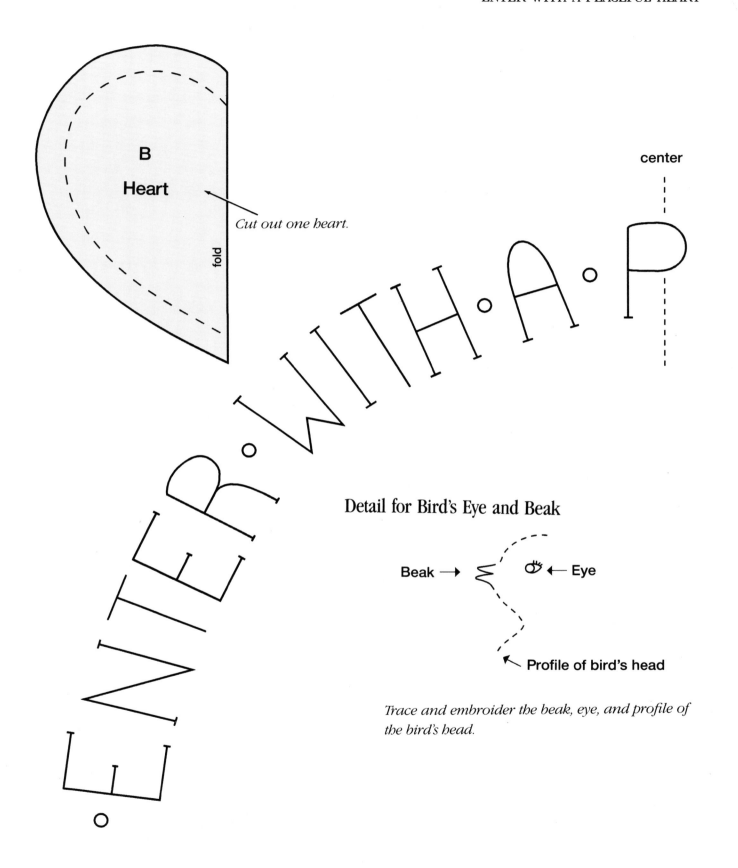

B

Heart

fold

Cut out one heart.

center

Detail for Bird's Eye and Beak

Beak → ← Eye

Profile of bird's head

Trace and embroider the beak, eye, and profile of the bird's head.

PEACEFUL·HEART·

center

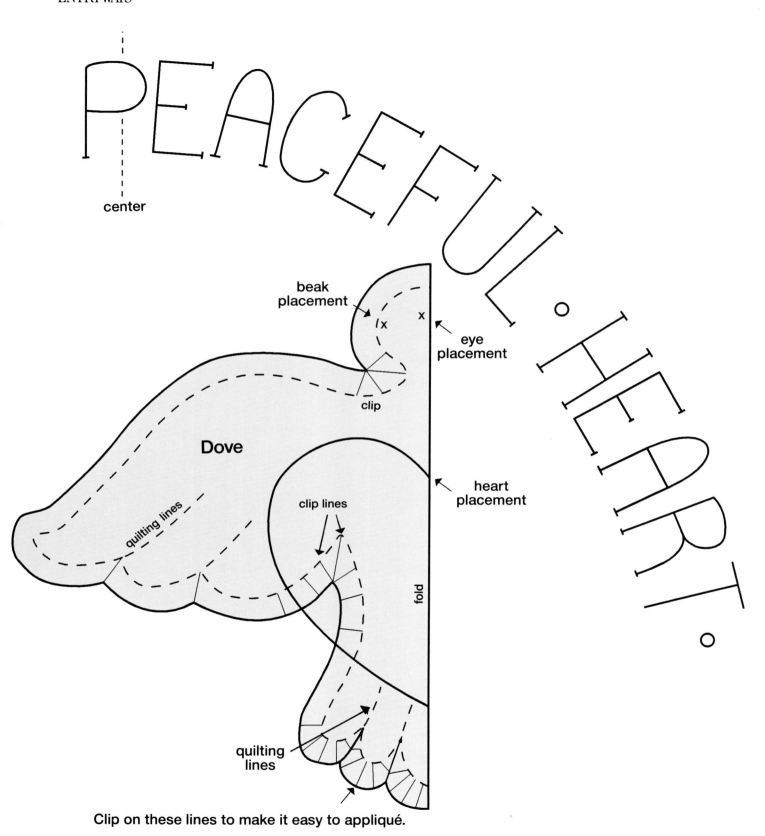

beak placement

x x

eye placement

clip

Dove

quilting lines

clip lines

heart placement

fold

quilting lines

Clip on these lines to make it easy to appliqué.

Attaching D Strip

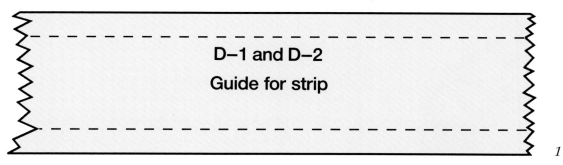

Cut one D strip on grain and one on bias.

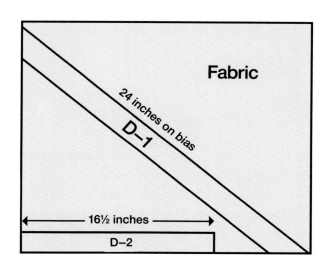

1. Cut 24-inch strip (D–1) on bias.

2. Cut 16½-inch strip (D–2) on grain.

3. Sew D–1 on first, around the top edge as shown.

4. Sew D–2, rounding ends afterward as shown. The measurement includes fabric overlap on the ends so that they can be curved to the shape.

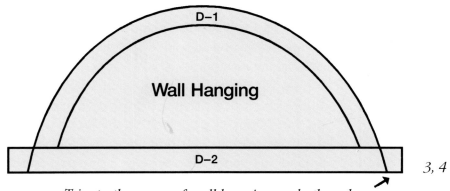

Trim to the curve of wall hanging on both ends.

RAINBOW WELCOME WREATH

Supplies

⅛ yard each of calico fabric prints in red, orange, yellow, green, blue, indigo, violet for letters, mini-star, and prairie point edges

⅓ yard of beige fabric with a light pattern for the wreath front and back

¼ yard of lightweight bonded Fiberfil

small bag of unbonded Fiberfil

15 inches of medium blue single-fold bias tape for miniquilt edge

1¼ yards of ¼-inch-wide gross-grain ribbon in red, orange, yellow, green, blue, indigo, and violet

bracket for hanging

quilting needle

quilting thread

Directions

Finished size: 12-inch diameter

Cut out two wreath shapes. Sew the ends together, leaving the bottom ends open.

Appliqué letters to the wreath, starting at the top center with the green *C*. The letter should be placed ¾ inch down from the outer edge and 1 inch from the inner edge. Work from the *C* shape, adding *O-M-E* on right side of *C*, and *L-E-W* on left side. Check the photo for reference if needed.

Next, cut out a bonded Fiberfil shape using wreath shapes as a pattern. Place the Fiberfil shape under the wreath, and quilt around all letters.

Prepare the prairie point edge following the steps and diagrams on pp. 30–31.

Now, cut out two more A wreath shapes for the wreath's back. Sew together the back's top ends, leaving the bottom ends unsewn. Set the back wreath to the front wreath, with right sides together. Stitch around the inner circular edge, and then stitch around the outer edge. Leave the bottom ends *unstitched* for now. Clip the unturned wreath around the inner and outer curve to eliminate puckering. Be careful not to cut the stitching when clipping. Turn the wreath right side out.

Place the front ends together, and from the wrong side of the fabric, sew them together by hand, using small stitches. The back ends should still be left open.

Stuff Fiberfil through the remaining back opening of the wreath. Use a knitting needle to pack the stuffing, creating a firm look and feel to the wreath. Once the wreath is stuffed, sew the back ends together, with the raw edges turned towards the inside of the wreath. Use small stitches so they won't show. Also, join prairie points following the diagram provided.

Prepare the bow and the miniquilt front shown in the assembly diagrams.

Complete the miniquilt, following these steps.

Cut out a 3½-by-3½-inch square of fabric and one of Fiberfil. Put the back, Fiberfil, and top together and baste. Quilt around the design of the star and around the B block. Bind the miniquilt's edges with single-fold bias tape. Follow the diagram provided for placement of the miniquilt on the wreath, and sew it in place.

Sew a bracket for hanging on the top back side of the wreath.

Letters for Wreath

Clip on diagonal lines for appliqué.

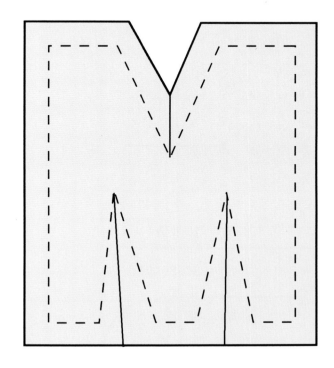

M *Cut one indigo.*

W *Turn M upside down; cut one red.*

For Miniquilt

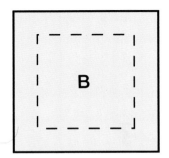

Cut four light and one dark.

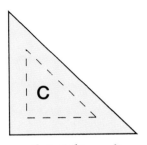

Cut eight medium and four dark.

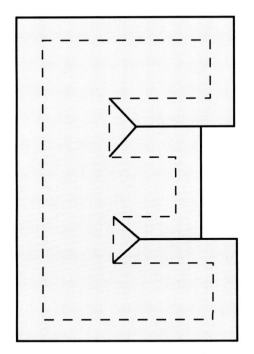

E *Cut two—one orange and one violet.*

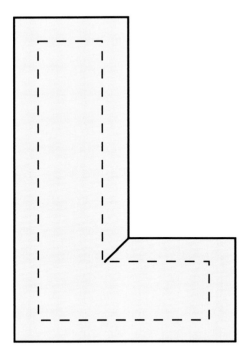

L *Cut one bright yellow.*

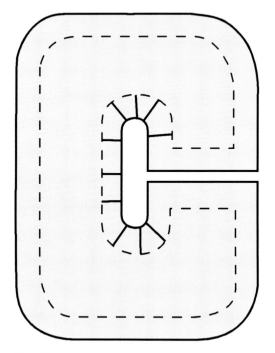

C *Cut one green.*

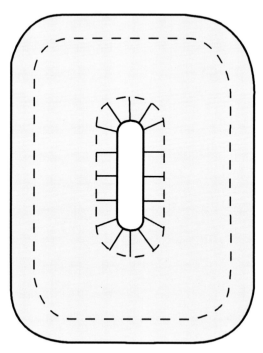

O *Cut one blue.*

Seam allowance: ¹⁄₄ inch

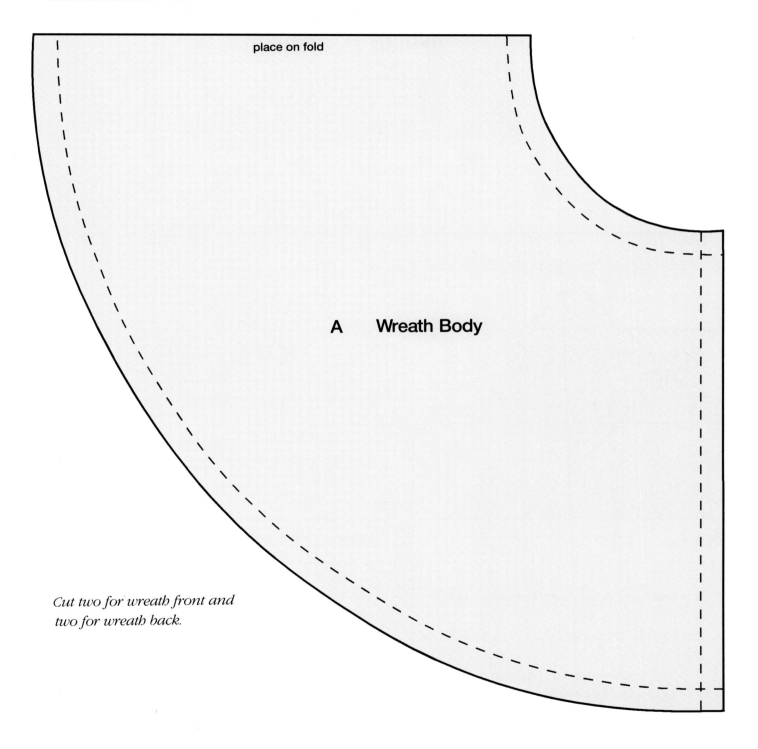

place on fold

A   Wreath Body

Cut two for wreath front and two for wreath back.

Miniquilt Assembly

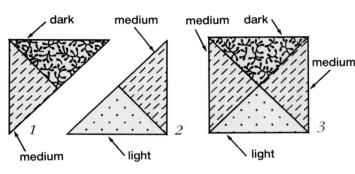

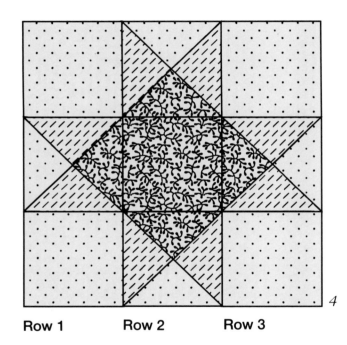

Row 1   **Row 2**   **Row 3**

1. Sew together a dark C and a medium C fabric.

2. Sew together a medium C and a light C fabric.

3. Now sew together the two pieces as shown. Make four of these blocks shown.

4. Note the color placement, and sew the rows as shown. Then sew the rows together in order.

Prairie Points Edging

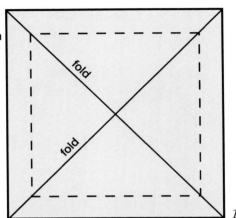

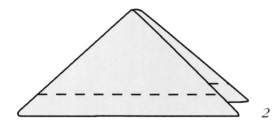

1. Cut five red, five orange, four yellow, four green, four blue, four indigo, and four violet 2¼-inch squares.

2. Cut out the points in the colors given and fold them as shown, producing a triangle.

3. Starting with red, pin a chain of points together as shown. The second point should be set in the fold of the first point about ¼ inch in. Follow the colors of the rainbow to make a chain. The length of chain may vary according to how much is overlapped. If the chain is too short, add a few more points.

4. Stitch along the edge with ¼-inch seam allowance, securing the prairie point chain.

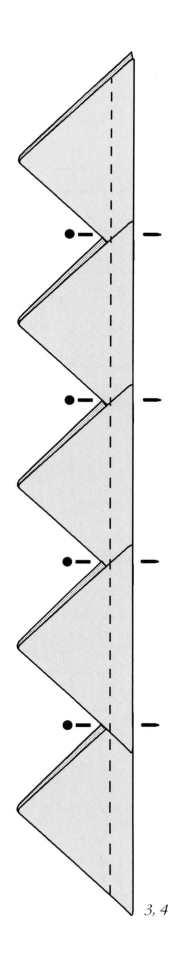

3, 4

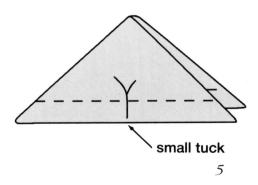

small tuck

5

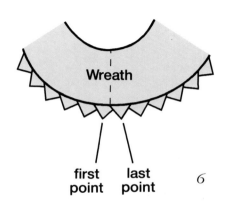

Wreath

first
point

last
point

6

5. *Sew the prairie point chain around the wreath front edge. (The bottom ends of the wreath will still be unjoined.) Because the wreath has a circular edge and the chain is straight, some points will have to be "eased" to conform to the shape. This can be accomplished by taking a small tuck in the prairie point, as needed.*

6. *After the bottom ends of the wreath are joined, remove ¼ inch of stitching, securing the first point to the edge. Join the last point to the first point and restitch.*

Ribbon Treatment

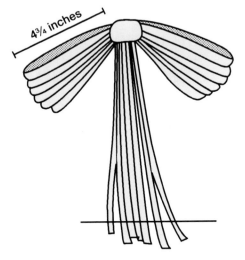

4³/₄ inches

Trim to make ends even.

1. *Bring together all six strands of ribbon.*

2. *Fold them in half to find the center.*

3. *Tie the ribbons into one bow with the loops measuring 4³/₄ inches each.*

4. *Trim the ribbon ends to be sure they are even.*

5. *Sew the bow by the knot 1 inch down to the center front of the wreath.*

Miniquilt Placement

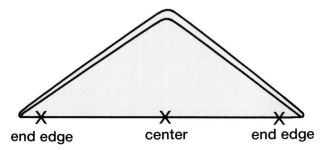

end edge   **center**   **end edge**

X's indicate where to hand sew the miniquilt to the wreath.

1. *Fold the miniquilt in half, to form a triangle.*

2. *Set the folded miniquilt's center on the knot of the bow. By hand, sew the center point (back fabric only) of the miniquilt to the knot as shown.*

3. *Now sew the miniquilt at the end edge point as shown. Be careful to only catch the back of the miniquilt when sewing it to the wreath.*

4. *Unfold the miniquilt. The edge of the quilt should protrude above the inner circle of the wreath as shown.*

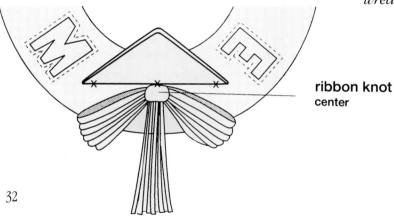

ribbon knot
center

STARS-AND-STRIPES MAIL BASKET COVER

Supplies

basket approximately 12 × 15 inches, oval shape
can of white semigloss spray paint
½ yard of navy blue fabric for B (cover's main top and
  bottom)
¼ yard of white fabric for stars and white stripes
¼ yard of red fabric for red stripes
2 yards of covered red piping
1½ yards of red print ribbon for basket's ties
skein of white embroidery thread
block of lightweight bonded Fiberfil 13 × 16 inches
quilting needle
quilting thread

Directions

Finished size: 12 × 15 inches

Because baskets are hand-woven, their shapes can vary. When choosing a basket, look for the best oval possible. But if the oval is slightly misshapen, it won't be noticeable with your cover in place.

Follow directions for making the center strip oval (A). Cut out cover B, and after centering, appliqué the oval stripe A to the cover. Trace the word *MAIL* to both ends of the cover as shown.

Using a small embroidery hoop and satin stitch, embroider the words. Appliqué two stars on each side of the word *MAIL* at both ends of the basket cover. Trace the stars to be quilted at the end of each of two star sets at each end of the basket cover. Sew piping to the outer edge of the cover.

Cut the ribbon into four equal parts, and pin it to the cover by the handle indents. See the finished cover diagram for placement. Pin the loose ribbon ends onto the body of the cover so that they won't accidentally get stitched into the seam. Put the cover back on the cover front, and stitch around the edge. Leave a 3-inch opening at one end of the cover for turning.

Clip the curves. Note the clip guide in the handle indentation areas shown on the pattern. Turn the basket cover right side out.

Next, cut a piece of bonded Fiberfil from shape B—cut on the stitching line, eliminating the seam allowance. Insert the Fiberfil into the basket cover, and close the opening with small stitches on the back of the cover. Baste the cover before quilting, making sure the Fiberfil remains flat inside the cover.

Quilt along the white stripes, around the outer edge of the cover. Also quilt around the appliquéd stars and premarked star shapes.

Prepare the basket by spraying it with white paint. Let it sit for at least 24 hours before using it. When the basket is dry, set the cover on the basket and tie it in a bow to the handle. Trim off the ribbon ends that are too long.

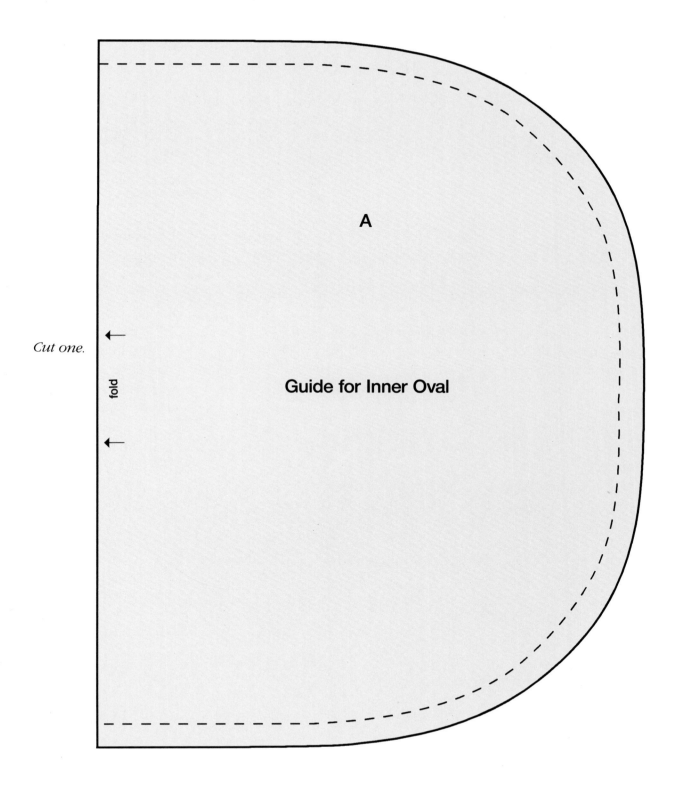

A

Cut one.

fold

Guide for Inner Oval

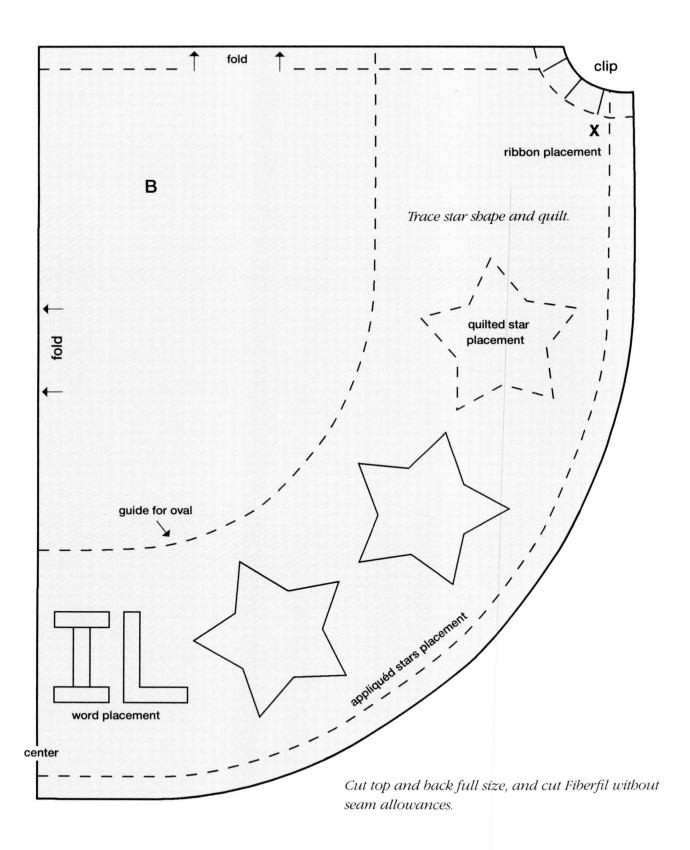

fold

clip

X

ribbon placement

B

Trace star shape and quilt.

quilted star
placement

fold

guide for oval

word placement

appliquéd stars placement

center

*Cut top and back full size, and cut Fiberfil without
seam allowances.*

Creating Stripes for A

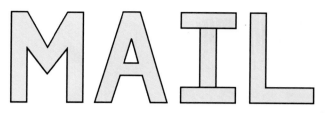

Trace to the center end on each side of the basket cover. Embroider with a satin stitch.

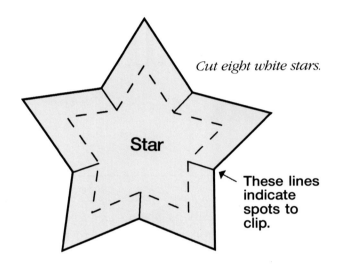

Cut eight white stars.

Star

→ **These lines indicate spots to clip.**

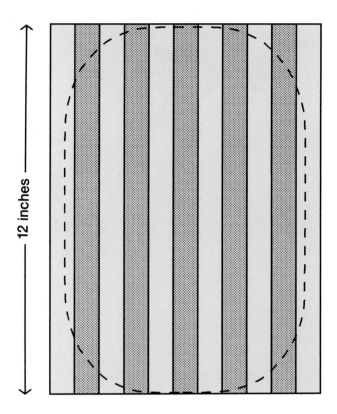

12 inches

Quilted Star

Trace four—two on each side. See guide for placement.

1. *Cut five strips 1¼ inches wide and 12 inches long in red. Cut six strips 1¼ inches wide and 12 inches long in white.*

2. *Sew the strips together, alternating red and white strips to form a block of fabric as shown above. Seam allowance of ¼ inch is already included in the width. Each individual stripe will be ¾ inch wide.*

3. *Center pattern A on the prepared stripes, and after pinning it down, cut the shape out.*

4. *Sew red piping around A's edge.*

37

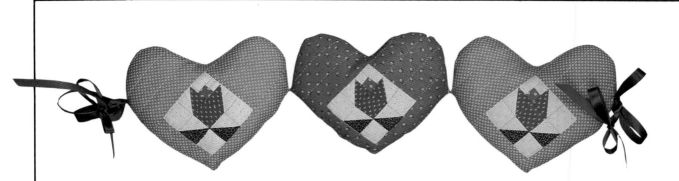

HEART-AND-TULIP STRINGER

Supplies

¼ yard of medium rust for E of the two heart fronts and for the back of each heart

¼ yard of medium dark rust fabric for E of the center heart

scrap of medium green fabric for leaves

⅛ yard of beige fabric for patchwork

⅛ yard of deep rust fabric for tulips

scrap of medium rust for tulip centers (C)

1½ yards of ½-inch-wide dark rust ribbon

unbonded Fiberfil for stuffing the hearts

¼ yard of bonded Fiberfil

quilting needle

quilting thread

2 lightweight circular brackets for hanging

Directions

Finished size: 8 × 25 inches (hearts 8 × 8½ inches)
Make three tulip blocks.

Sew the strips together to form flowers and cut out three patchwork E heart shapes. Make two medium rust hearts and one medium dark rust heart. Use one of the heart shapes as a pattern, and cut out three backs and three Fiberfil shapes. Set a Fiberfil shape under a heart shape and quilt, following the diagram. Quilt all three heart shapes.

Place the heart front to heart back with wrong sides together, and stitch around the heart's edge, leaving a small opening for turning. Stitch all three hearts. Clip around the edges of the hearts to prevent puckering, being careful not to cut into the seam line. Turn the hearts right side out. Stuff the hearts with Fiberfil, being sure to pack them firmly so that they will hold their shape. Close the openings of the hearts by hand, using small stitches.

Sew the heart edges together from the back side by hand. Note the point to sew the hearts together as marked on pattern E. Be sure that the darkest heart is in the center.

Cut the ribbon in half. Tie each piece into a bow with long ends. At the same place where the hearts are joined (only on the outer edge), sew the bows by their knots. Finally, sew a lightweight bracket to the back of each outer heart.

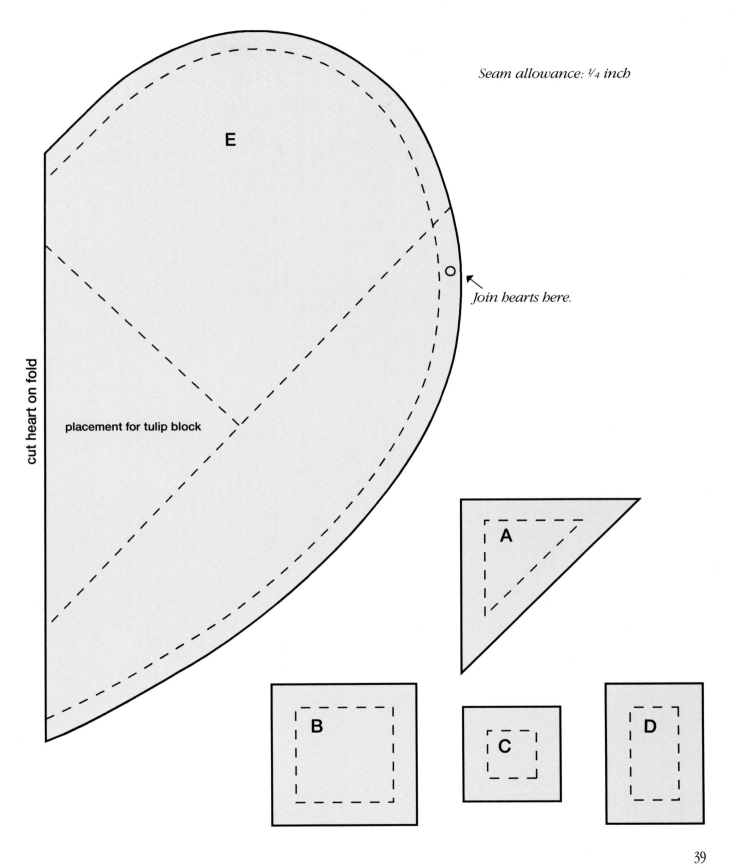

Seam allowance: ¼ inch

E

Join hearts here.

cut heart on fold

placement for tulip block

A

B

C

D

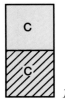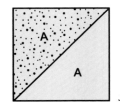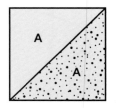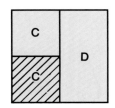

1   2   3

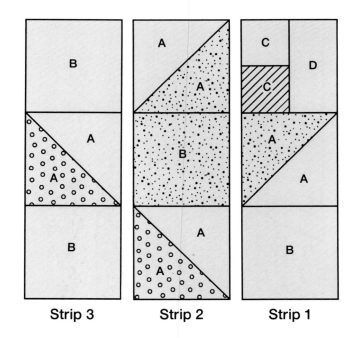

Make three tulip patches following these steps.

1. Sew a beige C to a rust C as shown.

2. To the right side, sew a beige D.

3. Sew a beige A to a rust A.

4. Sew the two blocks just made together. Then sew a beige B to the bottom edge, as shown.

5. Next, for strip 2, sew two A's together—one rust and one beige.

6. Sew two A's together—one beige and one green (same as E).

7. Make a strip with a rust-and-beige block on top, followed by a rust B, then by a beige-and-green block. This forms strip 2.

8. Sew strip 2 to the left side of strip 1 as shown.

9. Now make strip 3. Sew a beige A to a green A. Sew a beige B to the top and bottom of a block as shown.

10. Sew strip 3 to the left side of strip 2 to form the completed flower block.

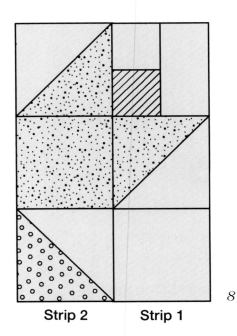

Strip 2   Strip 1

8

Strip 3   Strip 2   Strip 1

1. *To each end of tulip, sew a strip of fabric 3½ inches wide (same width) and 4½ inches long as shown.*

2. *Sew a strip of rust fabric 4 inches wide and the same length (12 inches) as for the tulip strip to the left side.*

3. *Sew a piece of rust fabric 2½ inches wide and 12 inches long to the right side.*

4. *Fold along the broken line. Now set the heart pattern on your fabric. Line up the tulip and tulip placement line on the heart pattern piece. Cut out the heart shape.*

5. *With your quilt marker, trace the broken lines 1 inch apart as shown through the body of the heart. Quilt around the tulip and the leaves.*

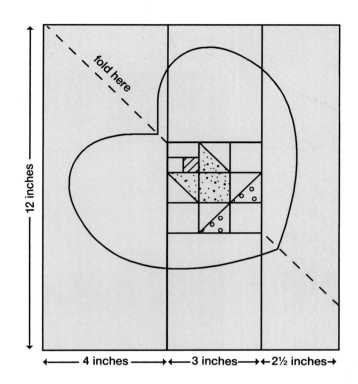

Note the direction the tulip is pointing.

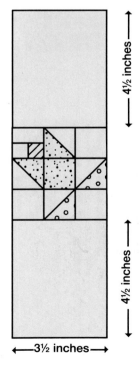

Quilting Detail

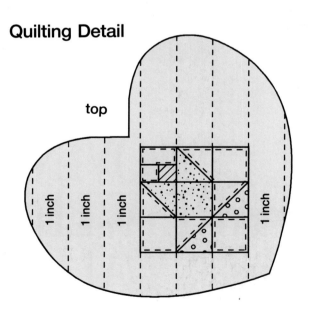

"LOVING FRIENDS ARE WELCOME HERE!" WALL HANGING

Supplies

skein of embroidery thread in coral and brown
scrap of white fabric for clouds
scrap of light peach for heart
scrap of medium green for B and leaves
⅛ yard of light brown fabric for fence, arbor, and gate
¼ yard of dark peach fabric for I strips and flowers
⅓ yard of light blue fabric for A and back
package of single-fold bias tape, dark peach
Fiberfil
2 light brackets for hanging
quilting needles
quilting thread

Directions

Finished size: 12¾ × 13 inches

Follow the steps for quilt top assembly to make the wall hanging's front, using the diagrams provided. Use the wall hanging as a pattern to cut out a back and Fiberfil block.

Put the back Fiberfil and top together and baste. Quilt the wall hanging around the appliqué shapes and along the I strips. Bind the edges with bias tape. Sew brackets on the back top edge of the quilt.

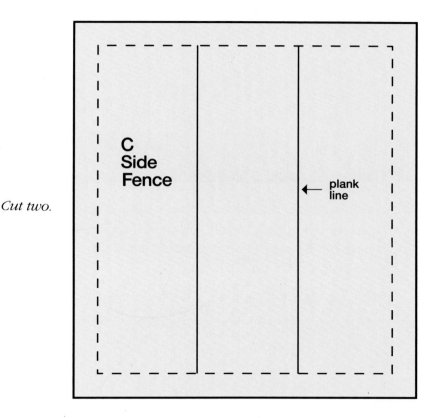

**C
Side
Fence**

← plank
line

Cut two.

Trace and embroider for box latch and hinge. ➤ ▭

Seam allowance: ¼ inch

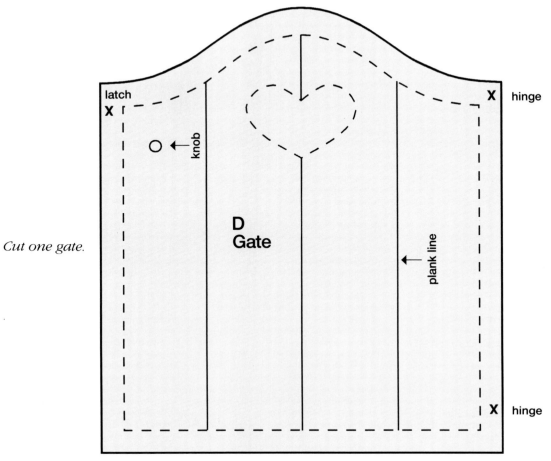

Cut one gate.

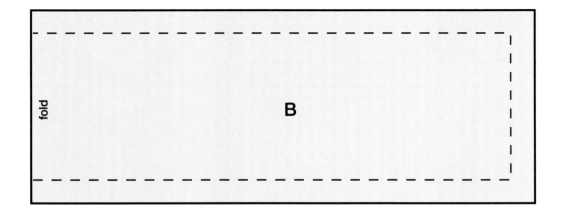

The flower centers, gate knob, hinges, and latches
are done in satin-stitch embroidery; all other
embroidery should be back stitch.

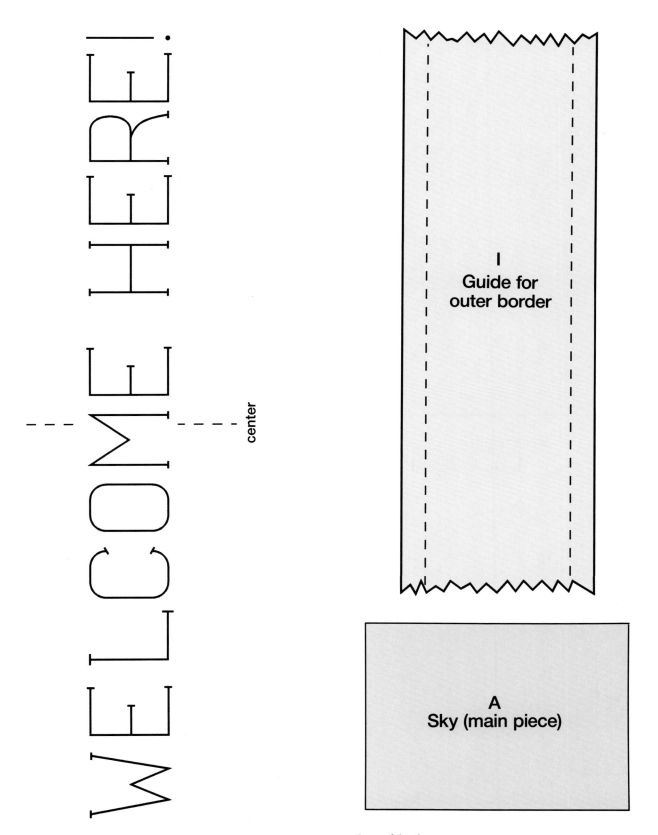

WELCOME HERE!

center

I
Guide for
outer border

A
Sky (main piece)

Cut a block 9 × 10½ inches.

LOVING · FRIENDS

ARE

guideline for arbor arch →

X
fence edge

X
fence edge

E
Cloud

Cut two.
Reverse one.

Leaf
*Cut two for each flower;
reverse one.*

Flower
Cut two.

Embroider
center

Flower Stem
Embroider with back stitch.

Heart
Cut one heart for gate.

Assembling the Quilt Top

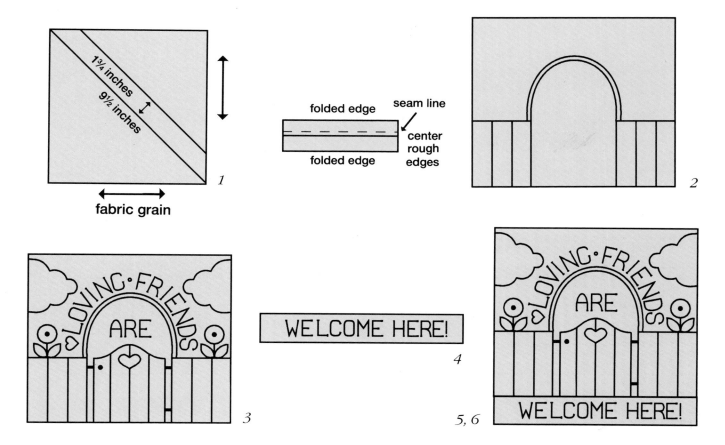

1

2

3

4

5, 6

1. Make the arch first. Trace on the fabric's bias a strip 1¾ inches wide and 9½ inches long as shown. Cut out.

Fold the strip in half. Stitch down the length of the strip, slightly off center towards the rough edges.

Now fold in half on the center line and press with a hot iron. The strip is now ready for appliqué.

2. Trace the arch line. Appliqué the arch.

3. Appliqué the fences. Embroider the fence planks.

Trace and embroider "LOVING FRIENDS ARE" and the heart. Appliqué the door. Appliqué the heart on

the door. Embroider the gate planks. Embroider the gate knobs, latch, and hinges. Appliqué the clouds. And, finally, embroider the flower stems, appliqué the flowers, embroider the flower centers, and appliqué the leaves.

4. Trace the words "WELCOME HERE!" on pattern piece B. Embroider the words using a back stitch.

5. Sew strip B to the bottom edge of the quilt top as shown.

6. Sew strip I to the top and bottom and sides of the wall hanging (see photo). This completes the wall hanging top.

CHILDREN'S ROOMS

*C*hildren are wonderful! Because we love them so much, we like to create handmade things for them. When we hear that a baby is expected, we take pride in making a gift specially for that new little one.

We often worry that handmade things for a child might be ruined or get dirty. But you don't need to worry. Simply make the quilts out of 100 percent cotton as advised, and you can confidently throw them in the washing machine. They'll come out good as new.

Two projects in this chapter are designed for infants—a whimsical diaper bag with a nine-patch surrounded by tulips, hearts, pins, and the words BABY'S BRIEFCASE and a cute bib that could be carried inside the diaper bag. The bib sports a bottle half full of milk and the words JR. GOURMET. The diaper bag, when not in use on the road, makes a good display when hung in the nursery.

The Child's Fantasy *quilt is a wall hanging that could work in a baby's or an older child's room. It combines two patchwork blocks, a teddy bear, and an ice cream cone in the middle. Around the happy border are kites, lollipops, and hearts. You could display this quilt over a dresser in the nursery or a child's room.*

The last project in this chapter is a pleasing patchwork pillow for a little girl's bed, "Sweet Dreams." The pillow proclaims, with the aid of satin-stitch embroidery, best wishes for a good night's sleep.

I hope your favorite little ones enjoy your quilting, and that these projects add charm to their rooms.

"JR. GOURMET" BIB

Supplies

¼ yard of pink fabric for front and back of bib
¼ yard of bonded Fiberfil
scrap of white fabric for the bottle
scrap of blue for nipple
skein of blue embroidery thread
skein of pink embroidery thread
1 yard of white single-fold bias tape
quilting needle
quilting thread
white thread for machine embroidery
blue thread for machine embroidery

Directions

Finished size: 8 × 10½ inches

Cut out the front and back of the bib shape and a Fiberfil shape as well. Trim the seam allowance from the Fiberfil bib shape.

Trace the words "JR. GOURMET" 1½ half inches from the bottom of the bib. Be sure the words are centered. Using a satin stitch on your machine, embroider the words.(Or hand-embroider them with a back stitch.)

Trace the numbers and milk level lines on the bottle. Machine-embroider the milk level lines using the small-width satin stitch. Hand-embroider numbers using one strand of embroidery thread. Next, set the bottle ¾ inch above the words and center. With a glue stick, secure the bottle in place. Machine-appliqué the bottle to the bib front. (Or, if you wish, hand-appliqué the bottle, but you'll need to add a ¼-inch seam allowance to the pattern.)

Now glue the nipple in place to the bottle top, and machine-embroider it to the bib front. Tie a French knot at the noted spot on the nipple.

Place the bib front and back with right sides together, and stitch around the outer edge, leaving the curve of the neck unstitched. Turn the bib right side out. Insert a Fiberfil bib shape into the bib. Baste the bib's back, front, and Fiberfil together along the neck curve.

For binding the neck edge of the bib, see steps 1, 2, and 3. Quilt around the bottle and the edge of the neck.

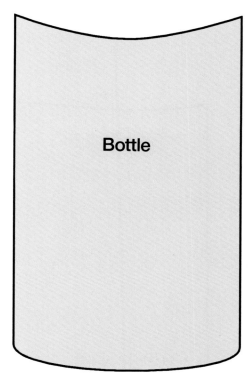

Cut one in white fabric.

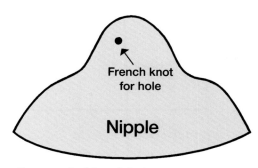

Cut one in blue fabric.

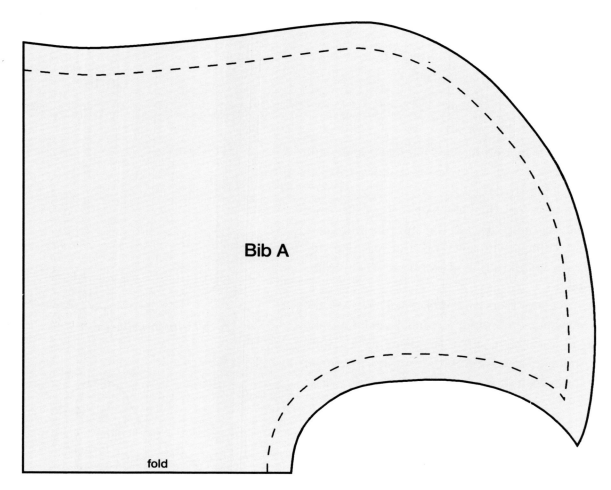

Bib A

fold

Cut the pattern on the line and tape it to Bib B before cutting two fabric and one bonded Fiberfil shapes.

Line up the edge of Bib A on the broken line and tape it in place.

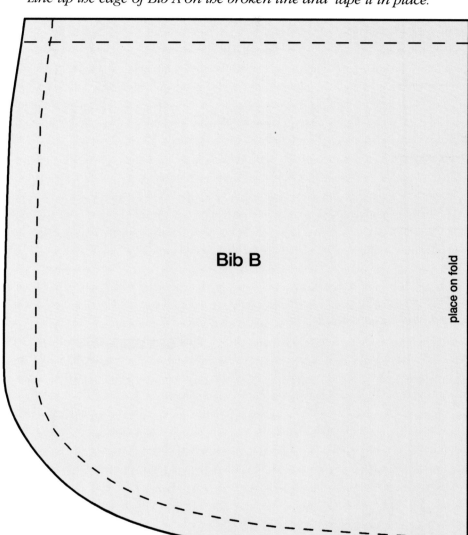

Bib B

place on fold

JR. GOURMET

Trace words and embroider.

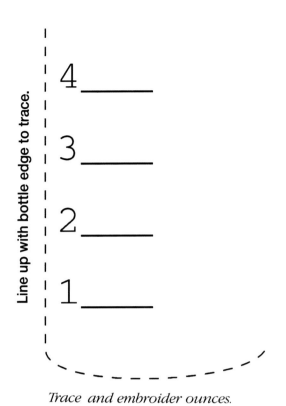

Line up with bottle edge to trace.

4 ____

3 ____

2 ____

1 ____

Trace and embroider ounces.

Neck Binding

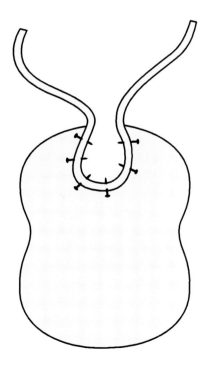

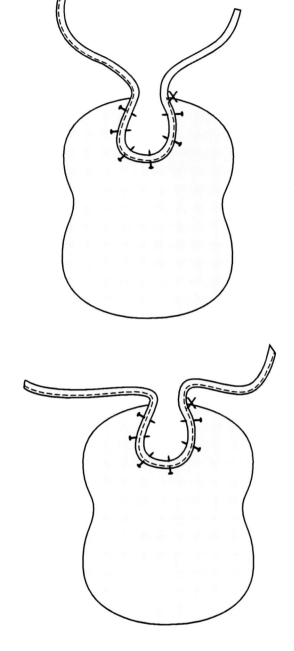

1. Fold bias tape over the edge of the neck opening and pin.

2. At X, top-stitch around the neck shape and beyond.

3. Top-stitch the other tie to its end.

"SWEET DREAMS" PILLOW

Supplies

¼ yard of white fabric for center block A

⅓ yard of medium lavender fabric for inner strip B and back

¼ yard of dark lavender for outer strip B

1½ yards, 2½ inches wide, of white cotton ruffle, gathered

Fiberfil for stuffing

square of Fiberfil 11 × 13 inches

skein of 6-ply embroidery thread—dark lavender for *SWEET*, medium lavender for *DREAMS*, light lavender for buds, pink for heart, and green for bud pod, leaves, and vine

small embroidery hoop

embroidery needles, quilting needle, and thread

Directions

Pillow size: 7 × 9 inches without ruffle

Trace the vine and leaves and words onto block A, making sure they are centered. Sew a light lavender B strip to the top and bottom of A and then to both sides of A. Sew a dark lavender B strip to the top and bottom of a light B strip and then to each side.

Use the pillow top as a pattern to cut out a back.

Then embroider with a satin stitch the words, buds, bud pods, and hearts. Backstitch for the vine.

Set the Fiberfil block under the pillow top and quilt around the vine, hearts, and buds. Also quilt the inner edge of the A block. Quilt down the center of the light lavender strip on all four sides.

Sew the ruffle around the edge of the pillow top, tucking under the rough ends so that they won't show. By hand, tack the ends in place without allowing the thread to show.

Put the pillow's back on the pillow's top with right sides together, and stitch around the edges, leaving a 3-inch opening for turning. Turn the pillow right side out. Stuff with Fiberfil. Be sure to pack the corners with a knitting needle so that they will stay firm. Using small stitches, close by hand the opening on the back side.

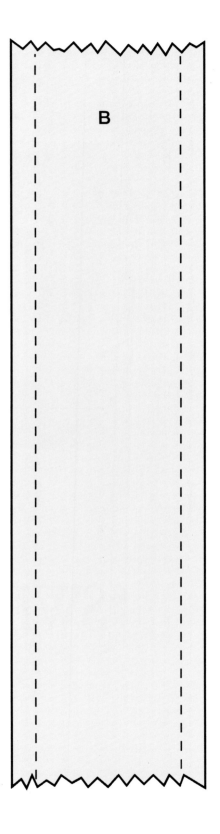

A   Pillow's Center Block

"BABY'S BRIEFCASE" DIAPER BAG

Supplies

¼ yard of white fabric

½ yard of light batting or Fiberfil

1 yard of covered pink piping

scraps of pink and blue fabric for nine-patch

scraps of blue, pink, and yellow for hearts, pins, and tulips

½ yard of pink fabric for back, pocket, and handles

½ yard of blue fabric for lining

yellow, pink, blue, and green thread for machine appliqué and embroidery

quilting needle

quilting thread

Directions

Finished size: 15 × 15 inches

Sew together a nine-patch using pattern piece A and following the diagram for color placement.

Follow the steps for front assembly, completing the bag's front.

Next, with a machine satin stitch, appliqué and embroider the hearts, pins, flowers, and words. See the photo of the finished quilt for exact placement.

Cut out a block of batting, a back, and two linings using the bag's front as a guide. Set the batting under the bag front, and quilt around the nine-patch, hearts, pins, and flowers.

Next, set the bag's back to the bag's front, with right sides together. Stitch around the edge, starting at the right top corner, continuing across the bottom and up the left side, leaving the top open and unstitched. Turn the bag right side out. Sew piping around the top edge of the bag.

Prepare the handles, as directed in the illustration. Pin the handles in place on the bag front and back as shown. Sew them in place. Following the illustration, prepare the pocket and sew it to the lining.

Set the two linings with right sides together, and stitch around three edges, leaving the top edge open. Do not turn the lining. Press the top of the lining ¼ inch out towards the wrong side of the fabric.

Now, cut another square of batting using the sewn bag as a pattern. Insert the batting square into the bag. Now insert linings into the diaper bag with a loose batting square between linings and the back of the bag. Also be sure that the pocket side of the lining is placed on the inner back of the diaper bag. Finally, stitch the lining to the top edge of the diaper bag by hand, catching the batting piece as you sew it to ensure that it won't move around in the bag.

For Embroidery

BABY'S BRIEFCASE

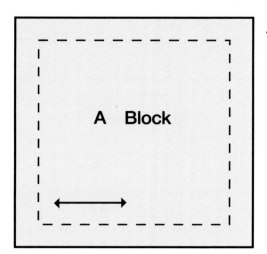

Cut four light, two medium, and three dark.

Sew nine-patch together.

Dk	Lt	Med	First row—dark, light, medium
Lt	Dk	Lt	Second row—light, dark, light
Med	Lt	Dk	Third row—medium, light, dark

Heart

Cut eight.

Safety Pin

Cut eight and embroider eight.

Cut four; two reversed.

Flower

Leaf and Stem

Embroider four.

Seam allowance: ¼ inch (no seam allowance on machine appliqué)

Front Assembly

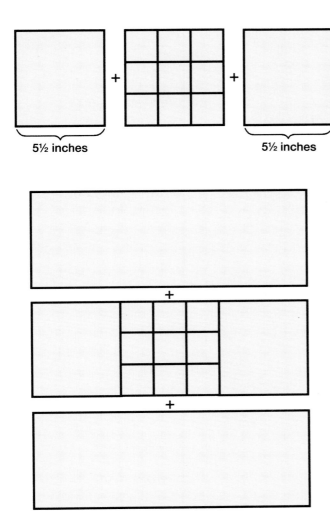

1. Sew blocks 5½ inches wide and the same height as the nine-patch.

2. Sew a strip 5½ inches high (the same width as the results of step 1) to the top and bottom edge as shown.

Pocket Detail

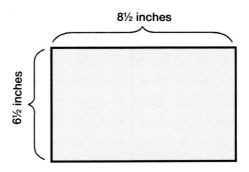

Do not stitch this edge to the lining.

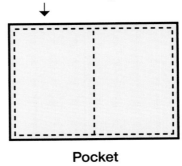

Pocket

1. Cut a block 8½ × 6½ inches.

2. Press under top ¼ inch once, and a second time top-stitch.

3. Press ¼ inch under around the remaining three sides. Stitch to the lining back around three sides. Stitch down the center as shown.

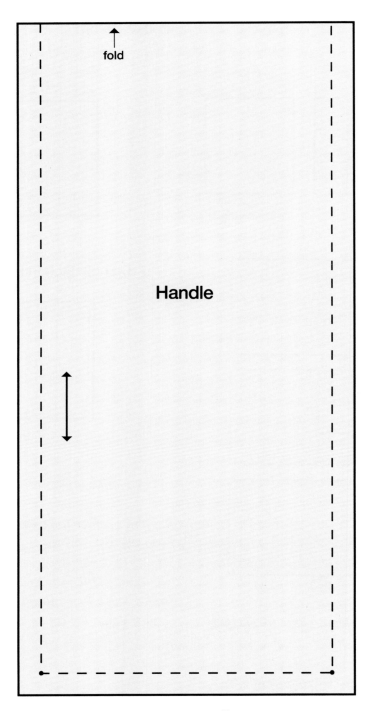

fold

Handle

Cut two handles.

Handle Assembly

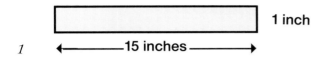

1 inch

15 inches

1

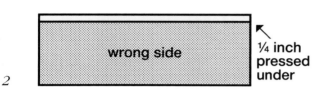

wrong side

¼ inch
pressed
under

2

1. *Cut two strips of bonded Fiberfil measuring 1 × 15 inches.*

2. *Cut out both fabric handles, using the pattern. On one long edge of each handle, press under ¼ inch as shown.*

3. *Wrap fabric around Fiberfil with the pressed edge slightly overlapping the rough edge as shown (pin to secure).*

4. *Machine stitch down the center of the handle, securing the fabric around the Fiberfil.*

3, 4

Finished Quilt Top (without handles)

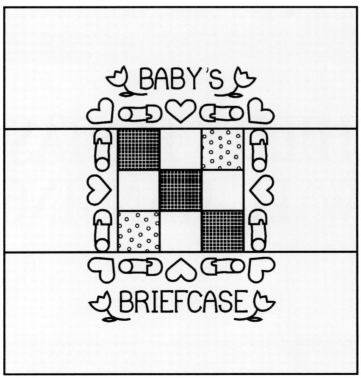

CHILD'S FANTASY WALL HANGING

Supplies

⅓ yard of white fabric for blocks and strips

⅔ yard of pink print fabric for back

⅛ yard of pink and blue print fabric for patchwork blocks

scraps of different small prints—blue and pink for hearts, lollipops, kites, bear's tummy, and ice cream scoops

⅛ yard of medium brown for teddy bear and ice cream cone

¼ yard of blue print fabric for C and C strips

1¼ yards of covered piping (pink, blue, or white)

brown, pink, blue machine embroidery thread

skein of blue embroidery thread for the bear's eyes

skein of embroidery floss for the bear's ears, nose, and mouth

block of lightweight batting at least 20 × 20 inches

quilting needle

quilting thread

3 plastic craft rings, ½-inch diameter, for hanging

Directions

Finished size: 20 × 20 inches

Make a pink and a blue patchwork block following the steps for block assembly.

Using a satin stitch, appliqué an ice cream cone to the center of an A–1 block.

Mark the face and ear details on the teddy bear. Appliqué the teddy bear to an A–1 block. Next, embroider the face and ear details using one strand of embroidery thread. Use a back stitch.

Now assemble the front of the wall hanging, following directions in the assembly diagram. Glue kites, hearts, and lollipops to D strips using a fabric glue stick. (See photo and diagrams.) Appliqué kites, hearts, and lollipops using a machine satin stitch. Sew piping around the front outer edge of the wall hanging.

Use the wall hanging as a guide to cut out a back and a Fiberfil shape. Trim off the ¼-inch seam allowance on all edges of the Fiberfil. With a hot iron, press under the ¼-inch seam allowance on all four sides of the wall hanging's back. On a smooth, clean surface, line up the back (wrong side up), Fiberfil, and top. Baste the three together, using contrasting thread.

Quilt the wall hanging, using outline quilting on all appliquéd designs and around the background of the patchwork blocks. Finish the wall hanging by sewing the quilt back to the back of the piping base all around. Remove the basting. Sew three rings (one in the center and one on each side) along the top back edge for hanging.

Patchwork Block Assembly

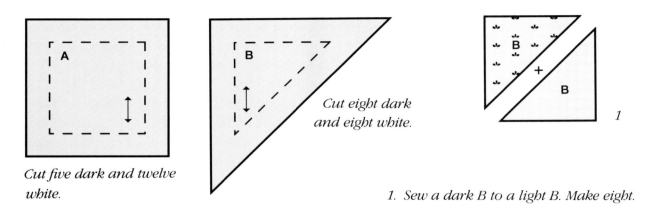

Cut five dark and twelve white.

Seam allowance: ¼ inch; machine appliqué designs have no seam allowance.

Cut eight dark and eight white.

1. Sew a dark B to a light B. Make eight.

2. Sew five strips as shown. Sew the strips together.

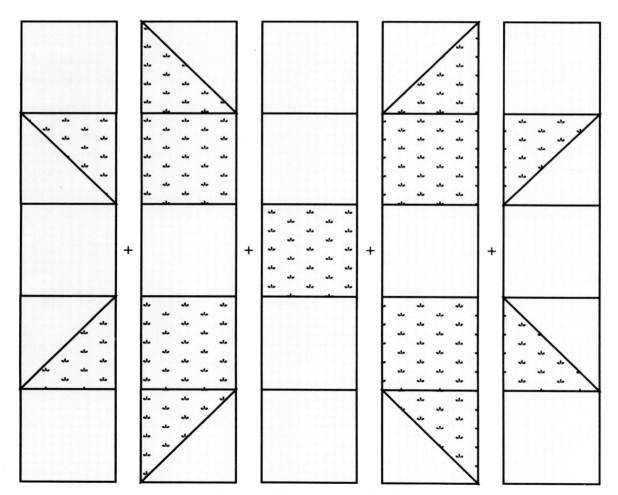

Finished Patchwork Block

Body of Wall Hanging

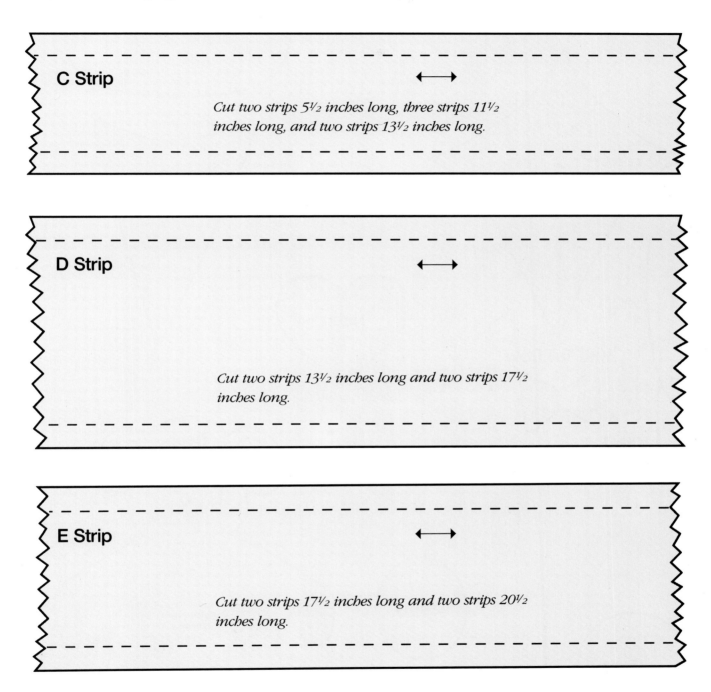

C Strip

⟷

Cut two strips 5½ inches long, three strips 11½ inches long, and two strips 13½ inches long.

D Strip

⟷

Cut two strips 13½ inches long and two strips 17½ inches long.

E Strip

⟷

Cut two strips 17½ inches long and two strips 20½ inches long.

1. For the blocks to appliqué, cut two measuring 5½ × 5½ inches.

2. Cut C strips for around blocks 1½ inches wide.

3. Cut D strips to be appliquéd 2½ inches wide.

4. Cut E Outer Strip 2 inches wide.

Appliqué Designs

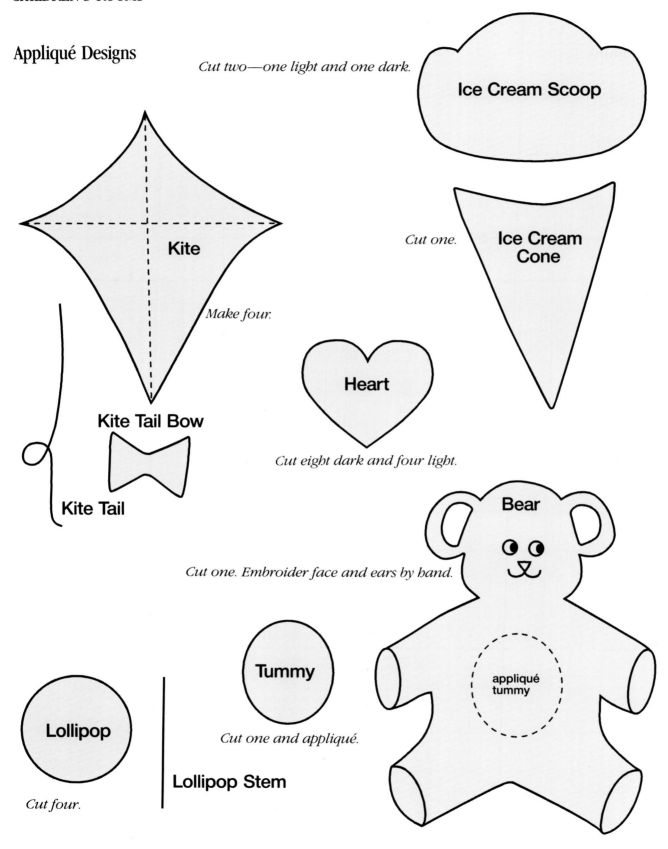

Cut two—one light and one dark.

Ice Cream Scoop

Kite

Cut one.

Ice Cream Cone

Make four.

Kite Tail Bow

Heart

Kite Tail

Cut eight dark and four light.

Bear

Cut one. Embroider face and ears by hand.

Tummy

appliqué tummy

Lollipop

Cut one and appliqué.

Lollipop Stem

Cut four.

Final Assembly

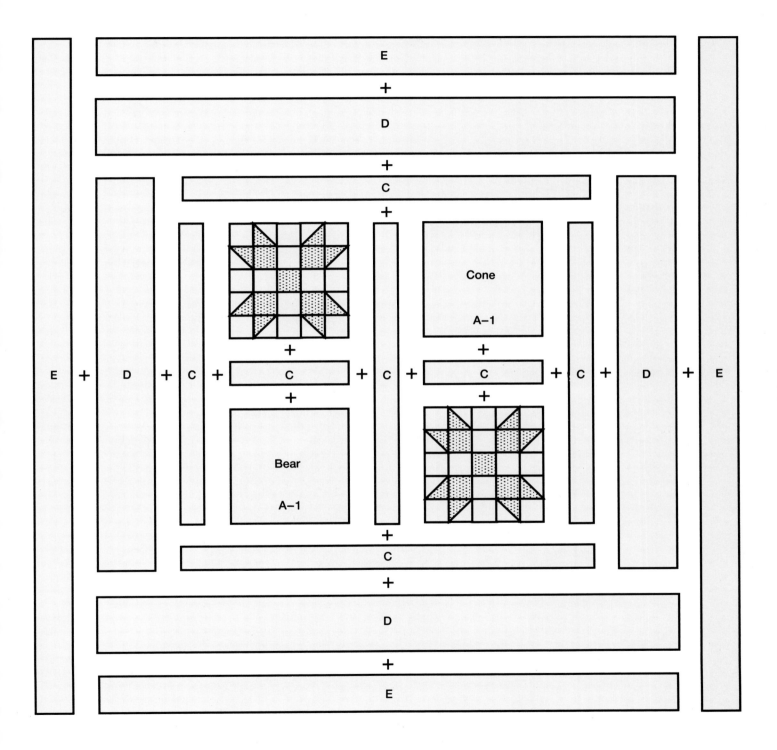

KITCHENS

*T*he kitchen is a wonderful place to decorate. If you believe, like many of us, that cooking is an art, then you'll want a kitchen that really inspires you. Decorate the room with handmade crafts of your own.

I have always liked the idea of having a bright and crisp red, white, and blue kitchen. So I've designed these kitchen quilt projects in those very colors. Of course, you can adapt these projects to the color scheme of your own kitchen.

I've included three pot holders—a Star *basic square, a* Four Corners *oven mitt, and an* Ohio Star *double mitt. I suggest that you make two of each—one for actual use that you can get dirty and one to hang on the wall for decoration. With lots of use, these pot holders won't look their best, but if you have a display backup, you won't worry about getting them dirty.*

The Country Baking Company *wall hanging suggests the mood of an old-time bakery. Visions of hot steaming apple pies set on a windowsill to cool may come to mind. Since a variety of methods—patchwork, appliqué, and embroidery—are used for this wall hanging, it should be fun to make.*

The last kitchen quilt project is a fun Chef's Hat. *You may simply want to make it for display, but if you are a serious chef, you may want to wear it while creating culinary magic.*

CHEF'S HAT

Supplies

½ yard of heavy white cotton fabric for hat top (crown) and pattern piece B

scrap of red for hearts

⅛ yard of navy fabric for A strips, back, and lining of hat band

⅛ yard of very lightweight bonded Fiberfil

skein of red embroidery thread

quilt-marking pen

quilting needle and thread

Directions

Finished size: 13½ inches high; expand hat band to desired size

Sew an A strip to the top and bottom edges of the B strip to form the hat band's front section.

Using a water-erasable marking pen, trace the word *CHEF* on the center of the B strip. Embroider the word using a chain stitch. Appliqué hearts on each side of the word, leaving ½ inch between the word and the heart.

Using the hat band front as a pattern, cut out a back hat band. Also, cut two additional shapes using the hat band front for the linings. Next, set the hat band front to the hat band back. Stitch on both ends to join the band, creating a circle.

Now cut out the hat's top (crown) main piece, following the diagram. Gather around the edge of the hat's main top piece or crown. Make two rows of gathering. Draw the gathers (by pulling strings on the underside) so that the hat's main piece will fit into the hat band.

Pin the hat's main piece to the top edge of the hat band, with right sides together. Stitch around the edge of the hat band, securing it to the hat's main piece.

Put the linings' right sides together, and sew the ends of the linings together on each side to form a circle. Set the lining over the outer edge of the hat band, with right sides together, and pin the bottom edges of the lining and the outer band together. Stitch the lining to the hat band.

Next, cut a strip of Fiberfil the same length and width as the hat band, without the seam allowances. Turn the hat inside out. Set the bonded Fiberfil strip on the back side of the outer hat band. Baste the Fiberfil to the hat band.

Pin the lining to the top edge of the hat band. First, turn under the top edge of the hat band lining. By hand, stitch the lining to secure it.

Turn the hat right side out, and quilt around the rectangle of the B strip and the hearts. Also quilt around the top and bottom edge of the hat band. Remove any remaining basting.

1. Cut out a piece of fabric 24 × 24 inches for the top.

2. Fold in half vertically to form a 12 × 24-inch rectangle.

3. Fold the rectangle in half to form a square 12 × 12 inches.

4. With a quilt-marking pen, draw a curved line from the top right corner to the bottom left corner as shown by a broken line. Cut along the broken line. This will give you the needed shape for the hat's top piece.

5. Cut two dark A strips 1¼ × 11¼ inches and one white B strip 2½ × 11¼ inches for the hat band. The hat size fits a medium head. Expand the size at the ends of the hat band if needed.

6. Cut out two fabric hearts and two paper hearts. Use the paper heart for paper piecing, appliqué (see the appliqué detail).

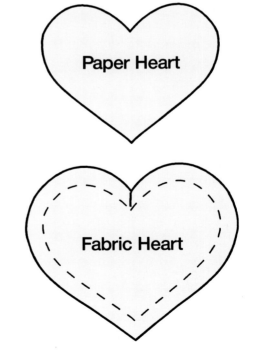

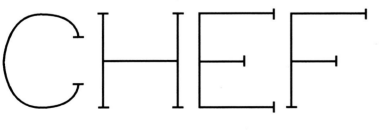

word for center front

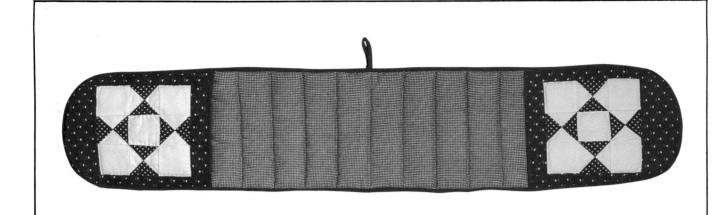

OHIO STAR DOUBLE MITT

Supplies

¼ yard of medium red fabric
⅛ yard of dark red fabric
⅛ yard of dark second red print fabric
⅛ yard of white fabric
1¼ yards of bias tape
½ yard of covered piping
¼ yard of bonded Fiberfil
water-erasable marking pen
quilting needle
quilting thread

Directions

Finished size: 6 × 30 inches

Follow directions for making the Ohio Star patchwork blocks. Make two. Next, make the outer mitt shape following the assembly diagram. Make two.

Using the outer mitt shape as a pattern, cut out two fabric and two Fiberfil shapes.

For each outer mitt shape, sew piping along top edge. Set the back mitt shape on the front, with right sides together, and stitch along top edge. Then turn so that the outer mitt shape is right side out again. Insert the Fiberfil between the back and front shapes. Baste the three layers together, lining the edges up exactly. Quilt around the white patchwork blocks so that the pattern stands out.

Cut out the F pattern on paper following the step directions on the illustration. Then cut out two fabric F shapes and one Fiberfil F shape. Set the three F shapes together (fabric, Fiberfil, and fabric), right sides out, and baste around the edge.

Baste the outer mitt shapes to each curved end of the F shape, lining up the curved ends exactly. Stitch around the double mitt shape ¼ inch from the edge to secure the outer mitt shape to the main F shape. Bind the edges all around the double mitt with bias tape. Mark the F shape for quilting. See below. Start lines at the point where the outer mitt shape ends. Quilt horizontal lines on the F shape.

Make the loop for the mitt by folding a 3-inch length of bias tape in half lengthwise and stitching the edges together. Fold it in half to form a loop. With the ends turned under, sew the loop to the under edge of A at the center.

Remove all basting threads.

Seam allowance: ⅛ inch

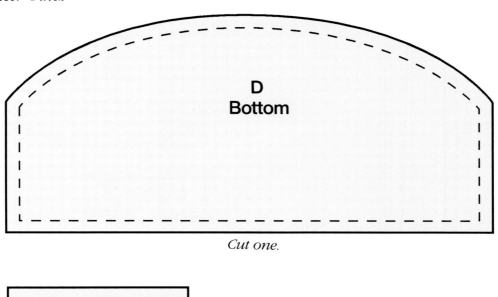

D
Bottom

Cut one.

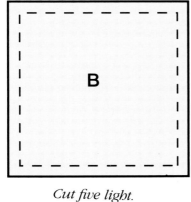

B

Cut five light.

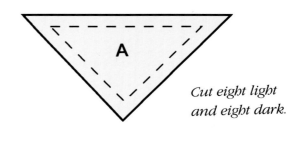

A

Cut eight light and eight dark.

The piece amounts given are for one side. Two sides are needed for the mitt.

Ohio Star Block

Seam allowance: ⅛ inch

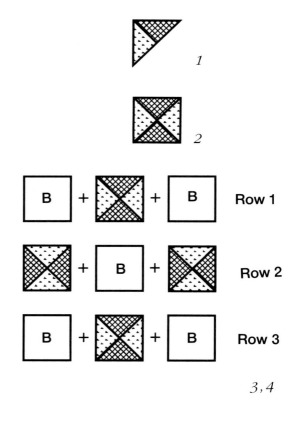

C
Top

Cut one.

E
Side

Cut two.

1. Sew a light A to a dark A to form a triangle as shown.

2. Then sew another light A to a dark A and sew the two triangles together to form a block as shown. Make four of these.

3. Sew together A–A blocks and B blocks to form rows. Note the position of the A–A blocks.

4. Sew the rows together to form the Ohio Star Block. You need two Ohio Star Blocks for the mitt.

Outer Mitt Shape Assembly

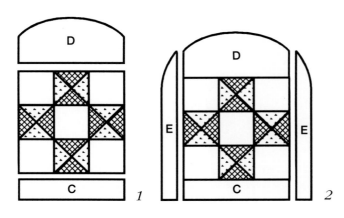

1. Sew the top (D) and bottom (C) to the top and bottom of the Ohio Star Block.

2. Sew sides (E) to each side of the patchwork block.

Making the F Strip Pattern Piece

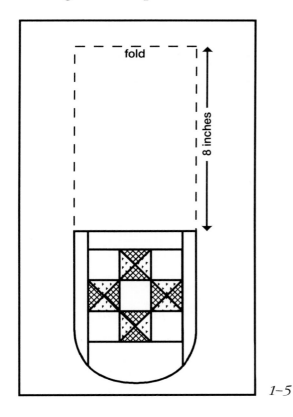

1. Use legal-size graph paper (8½ × 14 inches). Set the patchwork of the outer mitt shape at one end (see illustration below).

2. Using a pencil and ruler, draw lines towards the opposite end on each side of the mitt. The lines should be 8 inches long.

3. Trace around the patchwork outer mitt shape so that lines connect with the outer mitt shape.

4. Cut out the shape. The flat end of the pattern should be put on the fold.

5. Cut out two F strips.

Marking the Quilting

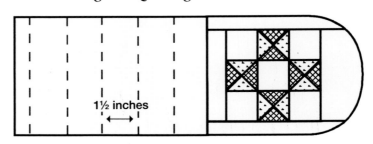

Mark lines for quilting every 1½ inches.

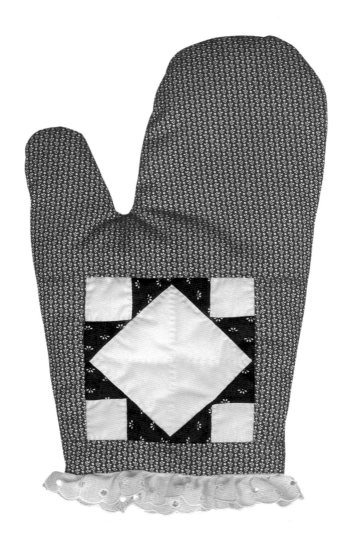

FOUR-CORNERS
OVEN MITT

Supplies

⅓ yard of red print fabric for mitt back, main fabric of front, and linings

scraps of navy blue and white fabric for patchwork

4-inch length of ½-inch-wide ribbon

12-inch length of 1-inch-wide eyelet lace

¼ yard of bonded Fiberfil

Directions

Finished size: 6 × 11 inches

Assemble the patchwork block (see steps by diagrams).

To finish assembling the front section of the mitt, first sew the side pieces (C) to each side of the patchwork block. Sew the mitt top to patchwork (A). And sew the mitt bottom piece (B) to the bottom edge. This mitt is designed for a right-handed person. If you want to make a left-handed mitt, lay the mitt top wrong side up when cutting out fabric. Check the illustration as needed.

Use the mitt as a pattern, and cut out a fabric back, two bonded Fiberfil linings, and two fabric linings.

Set the patchwork front mitt onto a Fiberfil mitt, and quilt around the white blocks.

Set the mitt back to the mitt front with right sides together, and sew around the shape, leaving the wrist open.

Clip the curves, especially where the thumb meets the rest of the hand. If the mitt is not clipped properly, the mitt will pucker. Turn the mitt right side out.

Next, sew the linings together; with right sides together, stitch around the edges, leaving the wrist open. Do not turn the right side out. Sew lace around the bottom edge of the mitt, turning the ends under so that they don't show.

Fold the ribbon in half lengthwise to form a loop, and stitch the ends of the loop to the desired side of the mitt's opening. Since the loop is for hanging the mitt, you can omit it if you don't plan to hang it.

Insert the other Fiberfil shapes into the mitt. Press the raw edge of the linings out to the wrong side of the fabric ¼ inch. Next, insert linings into the mitt between Fiberfil shapes, and pin the pressed under edge of the lining to the inner edge of the mitt. Hand-stitch linings to the mitt.

Seam allowance: ⅛ inch

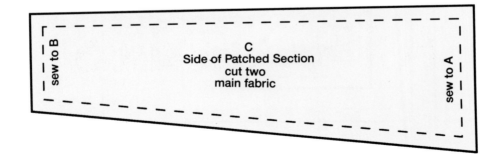

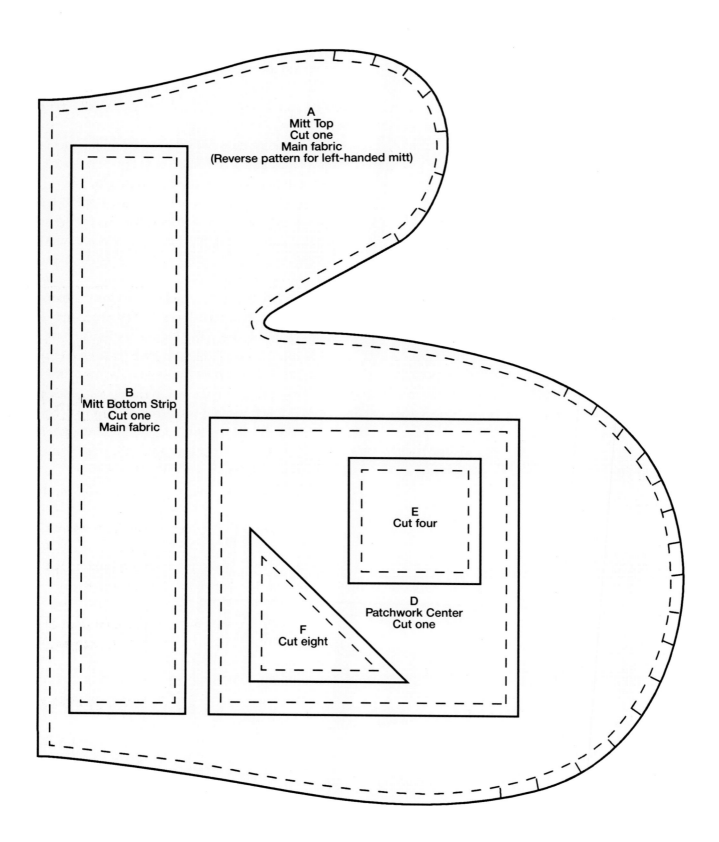

A
Mitt Top
Cut one
Main fabric
(Reverse pattern for left-handed mitt)

B
Mitt Bottom Strip
Cut one
Main fabric

E
Cut four

D
Patchwork Center
Cut one

F
Cut eight

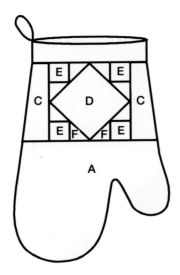

Center Patch Assembly

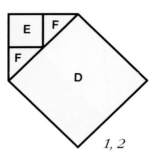

1, 2

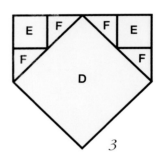

3

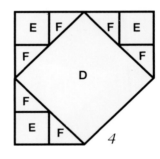

4

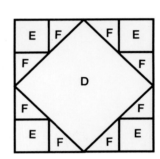

5

Corner Detail

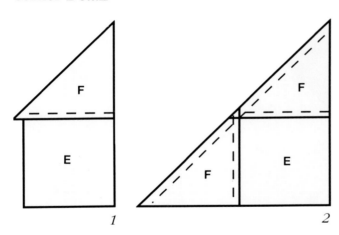

1   *2*

1. Sew an E block to an F triangle. The edge of F should extend beyond E.

2. Sew another F triangle to the edge of the E block and the extension will even out. The corner is formed. Sew an assembled corner to each edge of center block.

1. Assemble four corner pieces (see corner detail).

2. Sew a corner to one edge of the D block. The D block is set at a diagonal as shown.

3. Sew another corner piece to the right of the previously sewn corner on the next edge of the D block.

4. Sew a corner to the bottom edge of the D block.

5. Complete the patch by sewing a final corner to the bottom right edge of the D block.

STAR
POT HOLDER

Supplies

scraps of white, light red, and dark red print fabrics
   for A and B blocks
¼ yard of navy fabric for back, C, and D strips
1 yard of white covered piping
1½ inches of single-fold bias tape
small block of bonded Fiberfil
quilting needles
quilting thread

Directions

Finished size: 8×8 inches

Follow the pot holder front block assembly diagrams.
To the top and bottom of the block, sew a C strip. Sew
a D strip to each side. The front of the pot holder is
now completed.

Use the front as a pattern to cut out a back. Sew
piping around the edge of the pot holder. Stitch down
the edge of the bias tape to secure the edges together.

Make a loop of bias tape, and pin it to one corner
edge of the pot holder front.

Pin the back to the front with right sides together.
Stitch around edge of the pot holder, leaving a 2-inch
opening for turning. Turn the pot holder right side
out.

Cut a block of Fiberfil using the turned pot holder
as a pattern. Insert Fiberfil into the pot holder. Close
the opening by hand, using small stitches.

Quilt around the white blocks and light red blocks.

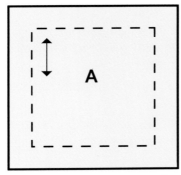

Cut four medium red.

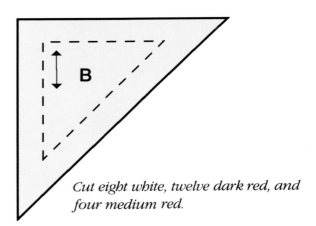

*Cut eight white, twelve dark red, and
four medium red.*

Seam allowance: ¼ inch

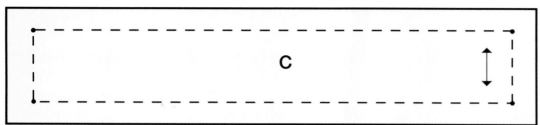

Cut two navy.

Cut two navy.

Patchwork Assembly

 1   *2*

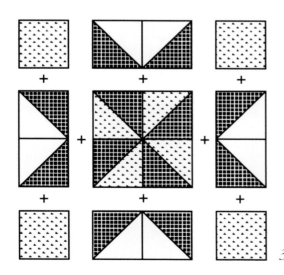

1. *Make eight white/dark red squares.*

2. *Make four dark red/medium red B–B squares.*

3. *Assemble the pot holder front block as shown.*

COUNTRY BAKING COMPANY WALL HANGING

Supplies

¾ yard of muslin fabric for back, labels, A, B, and C
  blocks

¼ yard of medium blue fabric for medium F and G

¼ yard of light blue fabric for light F and G

¼ yard of brown fabric for darker A strip and brown
  G's

scraps of 2 other brown prints for flour sack and pie
  crust

scrap of grey for pie tin and baking powder can

scraps of red print fabric for sugar bowl and apples

skein of red, blue, and green embroidery thread

1¾ yards of blue single-fold bias tape for binding

1 block of Fiberfil 13½ × 18½ inches

water-erasable quilt-marking pen

3 plastic rings for hanging brackets

quilting needle

quilting thread

Directions

Finished size: 13 × 18 inches

First, trace and embroider all words, using a back stitch. For label words, use floss—two strands for *FLOUR*, two for *SUGAR*, and one for *BAKING POW-DER*. For the words on the D block, *COUNTRY BAK-ING* (—dot—) *COMPANY*, use three strands of floss. Make the "dot" using a French knot and three strands of floss. Use three strands of floss for words on the light A block, *ESTABLISHED 1847*.

Trace and embroider pie vents using the satin stitch and three strands of floss. On the D block, on each side of the embroidered word *COUNTRY*, appliqué an apple and leaf, and embroider the stem of green, using one strand of floss. Note the angle on the illustration below. Complete the D block by appliqué-ing the pie top, crust, and tin in the center ⅓ inch above the words *BAKING COMPANY*.

Now sew a brown A strip to the bottom of the B block. Sew the A strip with *ESTABLISHED* (—dot—)

1847 to the bottom of the brown A strip.

Next appliqué the B–A–A blocks described below.

Appliqué the flour sack (centered) with its bottom edge overlapping ½ inch on the brown A strip. Con-sult the pattern diagram for placement. Use three strands of red embroidery floss and make ties on the sack, bringing the needle out at one edge of the tie and entering at the other edge to create a line. Appli-qué the label *FLOUR XXX* on the top center of the bag.

Left of the flour sack, appliqué the sugar bowl, handles, top, and top knob. Also appliqué the label *SUGAR*. Note that sugar bowl handles are made from small bias strips of fabric folded to ¼ inch wide and 1¼ inches long. Right of the flour sack, appliqué the baking powder can, top, and label *BAKING POWDER*.

Next, join the two main blocks (B–A–A–D) by sewing a C strip to the bottom edge of D. Then sew the B block to the bottom edge of the C strip.

Prepare the border. Sew a light F triangle to a dark F triangle to form a block. Make eighteen of these. Sew a medium blue G triangle to a medium brown G triangle. Make two of these, and then sew them to-gether to form a block. Make four blocks. Make a strip made of two F–F blocks, an E block, and two F–F blocks. Sew this strip to the quilt's top edge. Consult the illustration for correct color placement.

Now make two strips of the seven F–F blocks sewn together with G triangle blocks sewn to each end. Sew these F–F strips to each side of the wall hanging. The wall hanging front is now completed.

Use the wall hanging as a pattern and cut out a back. Line up the back, Fiberfil block, and front ex-actly, and baste them together both vertically and horizontally, using running stitches 2 inches apart.

Quilt the wall hanging. Use outline quilting on all light triangles on the border, and around appliquéd items in D and B, and around the edges of B and D. Quilt the background of D and B by marking a hori-zontal line 1 inch apart and quilting on those lines.

Remove the basting and erasable marking lines. Bind the edges and sew on brackets for hanging.

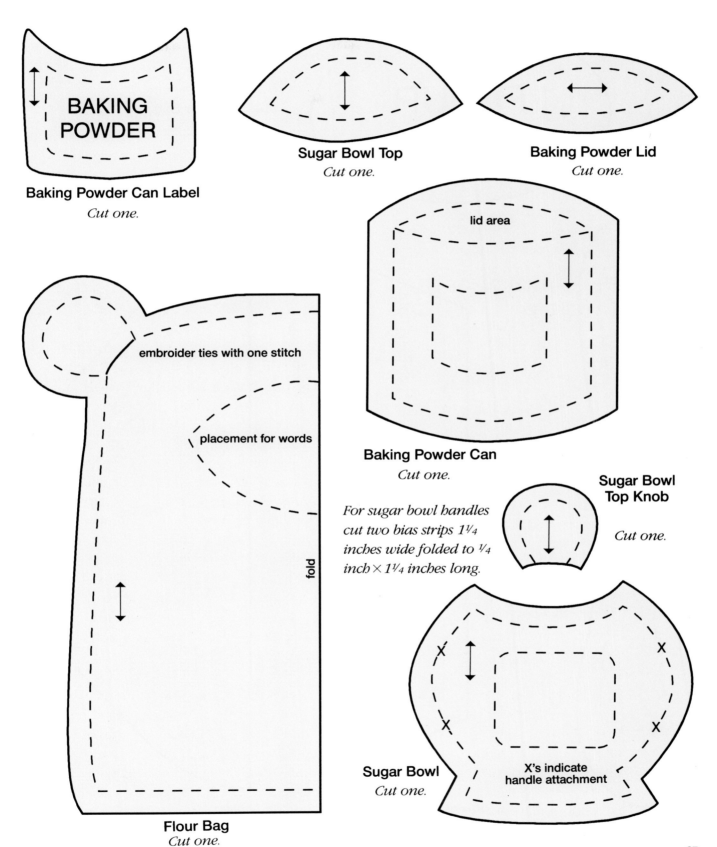

BAKING POWDER

Baking Powder Can Label

Cut one.

Sugar Bowl Top

Cut one.

Baking Powder Lid

Cut one.

lid area

Baking Powder Can

Cut one.

embroider ties with one stitch

placement for words

fold

Flour Bag

Cut one.

For sugar bowl handles cut two bias strips 1¼ inches wide folded to ¼ inch × 1¼ inches long.

Sugar Bowl Top Knob

Cut one.

Sugar Bowl

Cut one.

X's indicate handle attachment

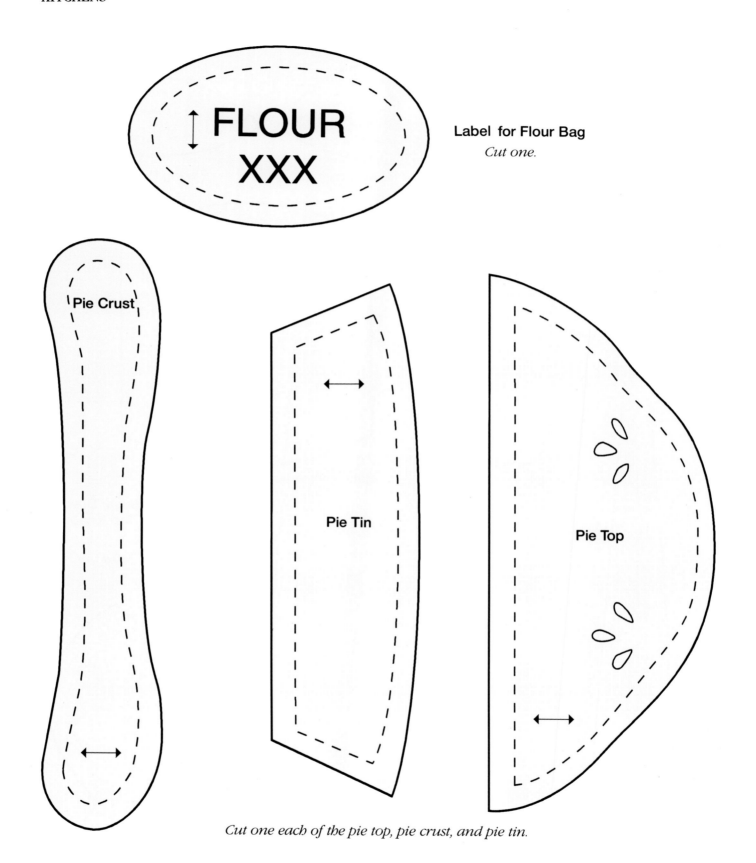

Label for Flour Bag
Cut one.

Pie Crust

Pie Tin

Pie Top

Cut one each of the pie top, pie crust, and pie tin.

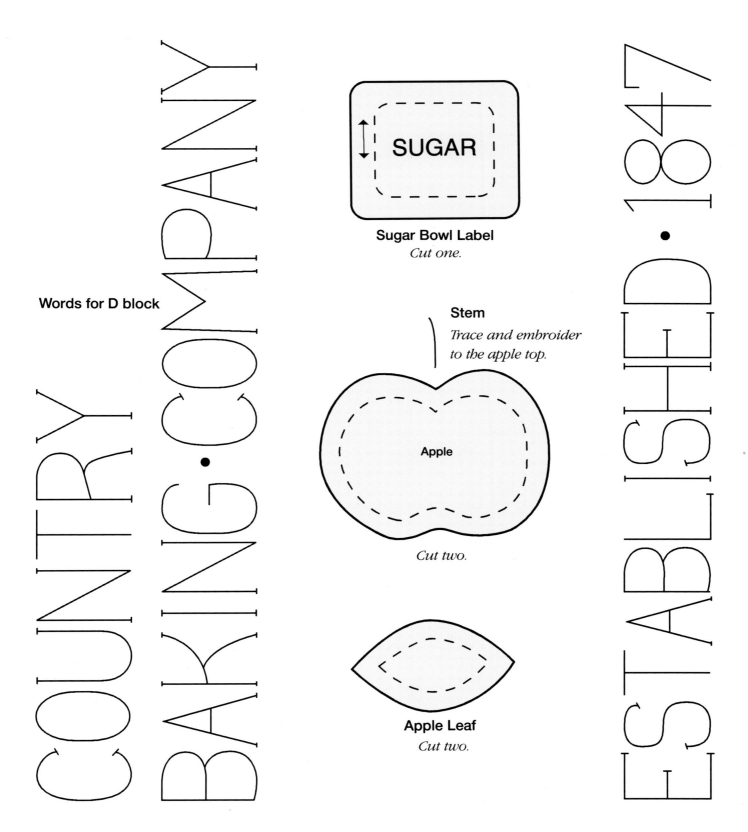

Words for D block

Sugar Bowl Label
Cut one.

Stem
*Trace and embroider
to the apple top.*

Apple

Cut two.

Apple Leaf
Cut two.

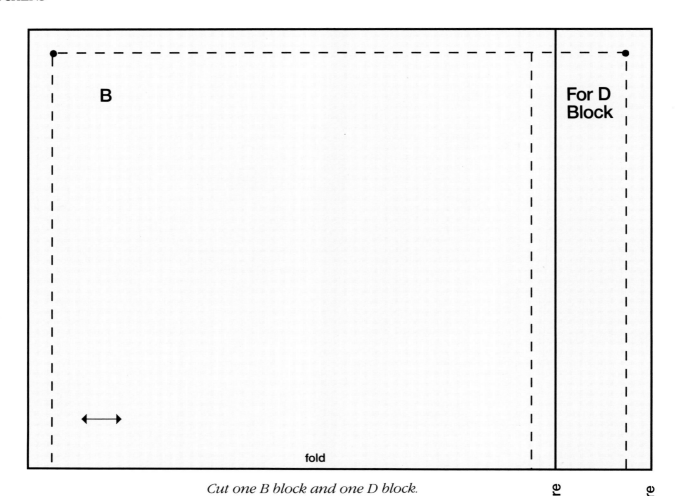

B

For D
Block

fold

Cut one B block and one D block.

B ends here

D ends here

E

For center
top border

Cut one.

F
For border

G
For border

Cut thirty-six.

Cut sixteen.

Cut two—one light and one dark.

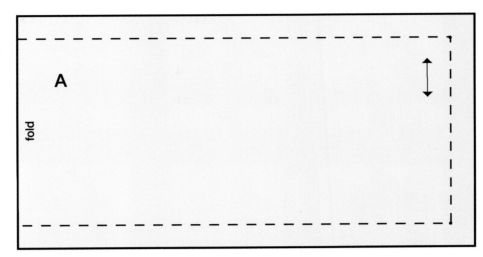

Cut one.

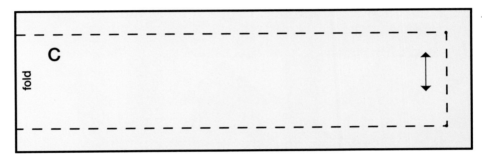

Assembly Diagram

LIVING AREAS

*T*he projects in this chapter can fit any number of places in your apartment or house—front room, family room, den, and bedrooms. And you may wish to move them around from time to time to change the look of certain rooms in your home.

The "Home Sweet Home" *wall hanging is a perfect design for a family room, where family members gather. This quilt, which reflects warmth and has a real old-fashioned look, combines patchwork, appliqué, and embroidery. "Home Sweet Home" could also look great above a couch or over a piano.*

The Log Cabin *tablecloth and pillow are a handsome duo that work well together. The tablecloth could be placed on a small table with the pillow on an antique chair beside it. The traditional Log Cabin pattern has been a long-time favorite of both new and experienced quilters. The Log Cabin blocks are hand-appliquéd to the tablecloth and pillow front—a new approach to a classic pattern. These two projects could look nice in a front room, bedroom, or family room.*

The design for the Hearts-and-Flowers *wall hanging comes from an antique quilt I bought years ago. I loved the design so much that I decided to adapt it for a wall quilt. The original quilt simply had flower wreath blocks. I've added the center heart and the border to a single block. This could work well in almost any living area, even the bathroom.*

The Shaded Evergreens *quilt I created when I lived in Washington state, since I love its many forests. I designed this quilt full of evergreens in many different shades and added a soft border of Wild Goose Chase triangles. I usually hang this quilt on my living-room wall, but it would look great on a bed with assorted patchwork pillows.*

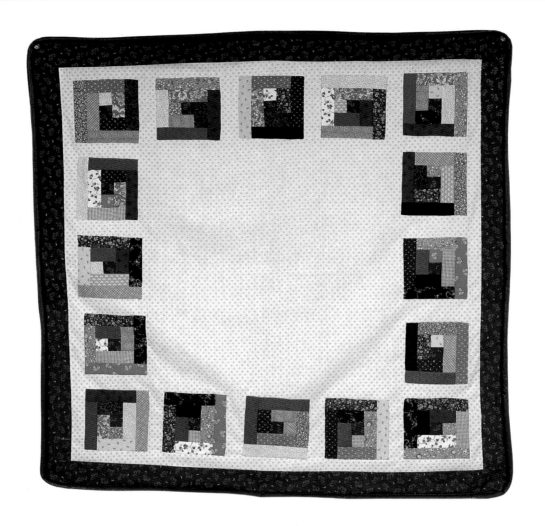

LOG CABIN
TABLECLOTH

Supplies

2 yards of light or white print for the body and back of the cloth

1 yard of dark green print for the border and strips in the small Log Cabin blocks

10 to 15 scraps of fabric prints in green, purples, and peaches

4 yards of cording with ¼-inch seam allowance

Directions

Finished size: 32 × 32 inches

Make sixteen small Log Cabin blocks following the steps in the diagram.

Cut out large blocks for the main piece and back of the tablecloth—31½ × 31½ inches. Sew the border strip to tablecloth's front—first to the top and bottom and then to each side.

Appliqué the sixteen blocks to all four sides of the tablecloth as shown. Sew the cording around the edge of the tablecloth.

Set the back of the tablecloth to the front of the tablecloth, with right sides together, and stitch around the edges, leaving a 3-inch opening for turning. Turn the tablecloth right side out and press. Close the opening by hand with small stitches.

Small Blocks for Log Cabin Tablecloth and Pillow

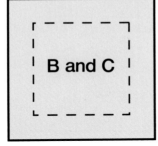

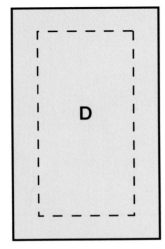

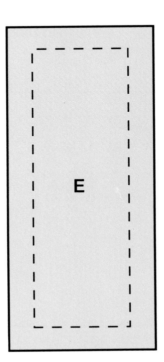

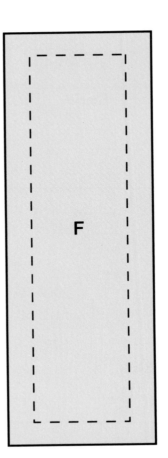

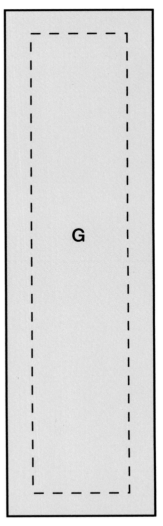

Small Log Cabin Block Assembly

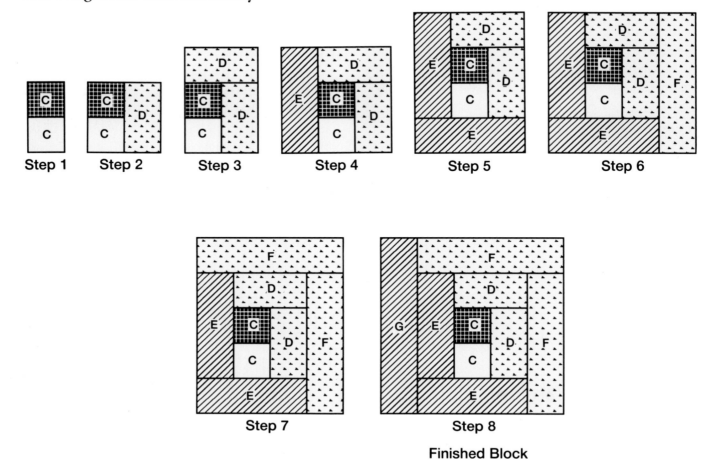

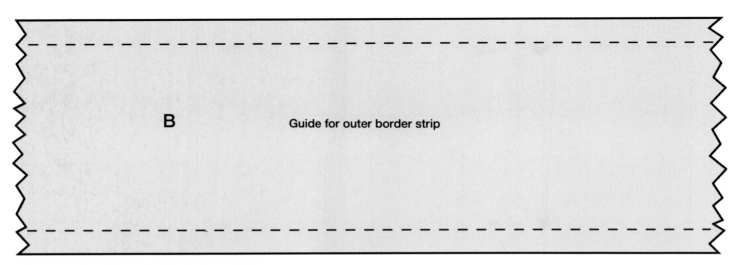

Guide for outer border strip

Cut outer border strip 2½ inches wide.

Log Cabin Tablecloth Assembly

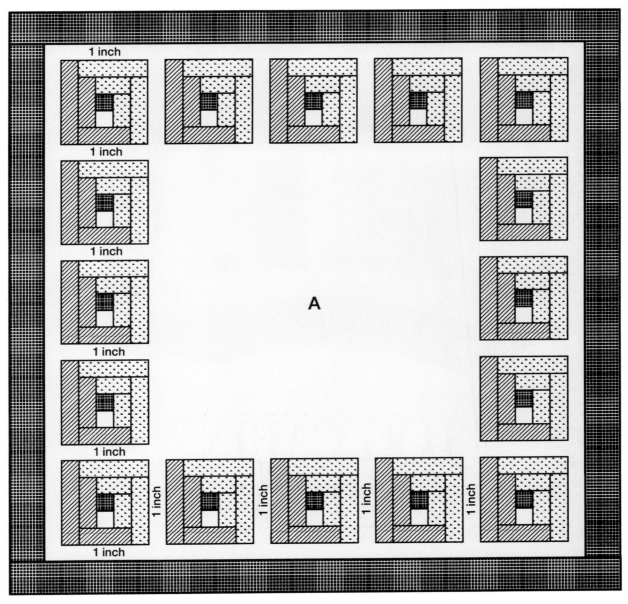

1. *Sew sixteen 5-inch Log Cabin blocks.*
2. *Cut one block of white fabric 31½ × 31½ inches.*

LOG CABIN
PILLOW

Supplies

½ yard of white or light print fabric for the front and back

scraps of fabric in purples, peaches, and greens

pound of unbonded Fiberfil for stuffing

15½ × 15½-inch block of lightweight bonded Fiberfil

2 yards of cording with seam allowance

quilting needles

quilting thread

Directions

Finished size: 15 × 15 inches, excluding ruffle

Make four small Log Cabin blocks. Appliqué the blocks to the pillow front, following the diagram for placement.

Place the Fiberfil block under the appliquéd pillow top, and quilt around the centers and edges of the Log Cabin blocks. Sew cording around the edge of the pillow.

Sew the pillow back to the pillow front, leaving a 3-inch opening for turning. Turn the pillow right side out; then stuff it. Use a knitting needle to pack the pillow's corners. Close the opening by hand with small stitches on the back side of the pillow.

Log Cabin Pillow Assembly

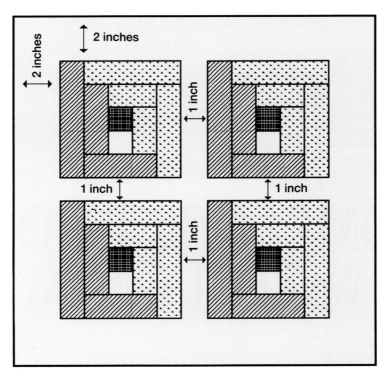

Cut a square 15½ × 15½ inches. Appliqué four Log Cabin blocks 1 inch apart to the background.

"HOME SWEET HOME" WALL HANGING

Supplies

⅓ yard of white fabric

⅛ yard of five print fabrics—dark cranberry, medium cranberry, light blue, medium blue, and dark blue

skeins of embroidery thread—medium blue (2), dark cranberry (1), and medium green (1)

scrap of green fabric for leaves

⅓ yard of lightweight bonded Fiberfil

⅓ yard of fabric for back

package of covered cranberry piping

quilting needle

quilting thread

water-erasable quilt-marking pen

embroidery hoop

2 light circular brackets for hanging

Directions

Finished size: 20 × 20 inches

Follow the assembly diagram for the wall hanging's top.

Using the wall hanging front as a pattern, cut out a Fiberfil shape and a back. Sew piping around the front edge. Place together the back, Fiberfil, and front, and baste the three both vertically and horizontally.

Quilt around the blocks and letters using outline quilting. See the diagrams given for quilting patterns on D blocks.

Turn the wall hanging over, and from the back side, turn the back edges under ¼ inch all around. By hand, sew the back's hem to the piping on the back side.

Remove the basting thread. Attach brackets to the top back edges for hanging.

"Home Sweet Home" Templates

Patchwork seam allowance: ¼ inch
Appliqué seam allowance: ⅛ inch

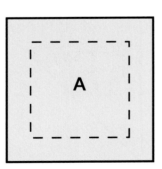

Cut out eight light and eight dark 1½-inch-square A blocks.

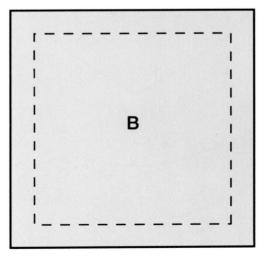

Cut out eight light, sixteen medium, sixteen dark, and eight very dark 2½-inch-square B blocks.

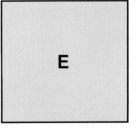

Cut out a white 8½-inch square for one E block.

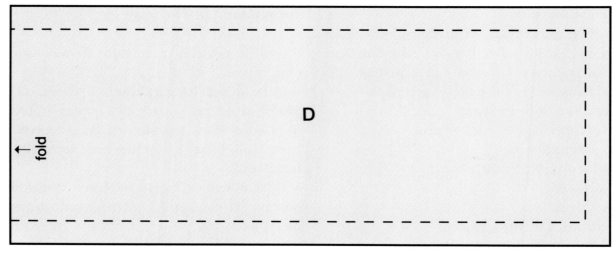

Cut four.

Appliqué and Embroidery for Bottom D Strip

Seam allowance: ⅛ inch

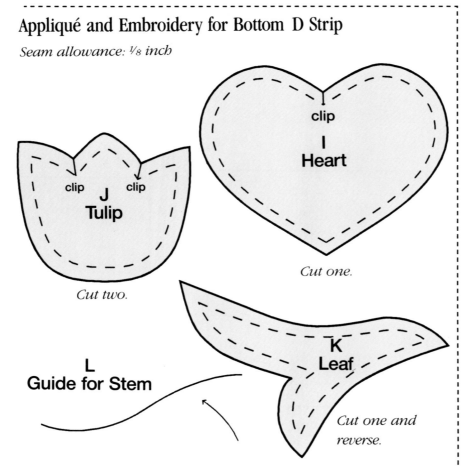

J Tulip

clip   clip

Cut two.

clip

I Heart

Cut one.

K Leaf

Cut one and reverse.

L Guide for Stem

Trace one and reverse. Embroider with chain stitch.

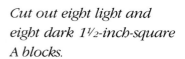

C

Cut out eight light and eight dark 1½-inch-square A blocks.

Embroider with satin stitch onto Block D. Make two "HOME"s.

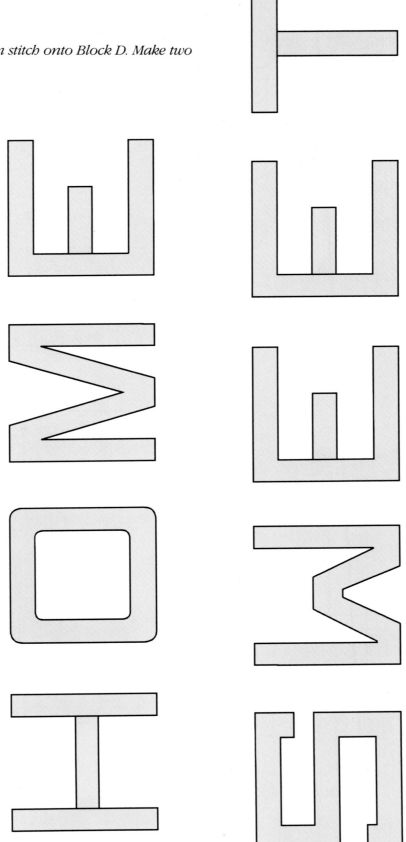

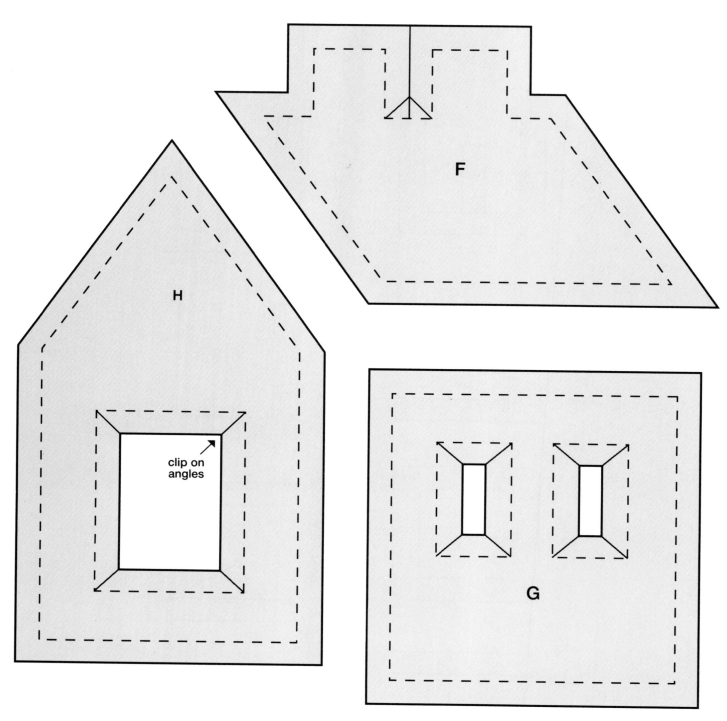

*Cut one each of pieces F, G, and H. Clip on
diagonal lines for appliqué.*

1. *On white cotton fabric, trace the words on three D strips. Centered within the strips, trace "HOME" on two strips and "SWEET" on the third as shown. Then, using a satin stitch, embroider the words just traced. Cut out the D shapes.*

2. *Now cut out one more D shape, and, using the guide below, trace the placement of the appliqué and embroidery. Appliqué the tulip and leaves, then the heart. Using a chain stitch, embroider the stem. (Reverse the tulip for the other half of D.)*

3. *Trace the house shape (centered) to block E. Then appliqué the roof, front, and side of the house (H, F, G).*

4. *Next, using medium fabric and dark fabric, sew together four A blocks so that they look like this. Make four of these.*

5. *Sew together two dark and two white C triangles to form a block like this. Make four of these.*

Repeat using two dark and two light triangles as shown. Make four of these.

6. *Now sew together four B blocks of varying color value. Make two of these strips.*

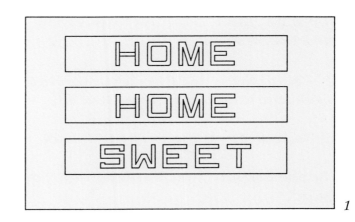

1

2

Placement for House Appliqué

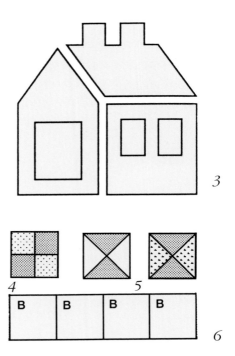

3

4

5

6

7. *Sew a B chain to the top and bottom edges of the E block as shown.*

8. *Make a chain of four B blocks, with C triangle blocks sewn to each end as shown. Make two.*

9. *Sew these strips to the top of the house block.*

10. *Sew the D strip "SWEET" to the top edge of the piece.*

11. *Sew the D strip with heart and tulips to the bottom edge of the piece.*

12. *To each end of the "HOME" D strip, sew an A block square (see step 4). Do this to both "HOME" D strips.*

13. *Sew a "HOME" D strip (with A block) to each side of the wall hanging as shown.*

14. *Next, sew together a chain of various colors of B squares, eight in all. Make two. Sew to the sides of the wall hanging.*

15. *Sew together two more chains of eight B blocks. To each end of these, sew a C triangle block (from step 5). Sew these strips to the top and bottom of the wall hanging (see assembled front illustration).*

Quilting Detail

1. *Here is the quilting design for each end of block D with "HOME" in it. Trace to the blank sections of D next to "HOME" on both sides.*

2. *Use this quilting design for D blocks, with "SWEET." Trace to each end of "SWEET," and quilt to fill space.*

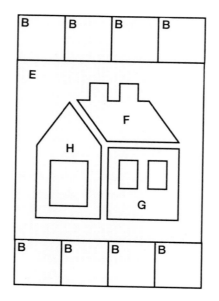

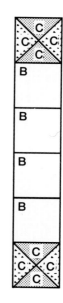

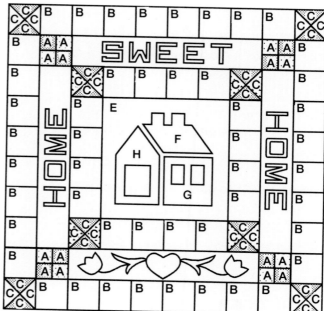

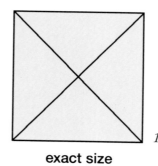

exact size   1

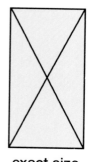

exact size   2

HEARTS-AND-FLOWERS WALL HANGING

Supplies

1 yard of medium green print fabric for back

½ yard of green fabric for A strips and half of leaves

⅛ yard of second green print fabric for remaining leaves

⅓ yard of white fabric for B strips and C center block

scrap of green pin-dot fabric for vine in center block

¼ yard of third green print fabric for vines on B strip

¼ yard of light lavender fabric for hearts on B strip

¼ yard of second light lavender for heart on C block

¼ yard of dark lavender print for flowers on B strip

block of lightweight bonded Fiberfil 31½ × 31½ inches

water-erasable quilt-marking pen

quilting needles

quilting thread

Directions

Finished size: 30½ × 30½ inches

Appliqué the C block first. Find the exact center of the C block by folding it in half to form a rectangle and folding the rectangle in half a second time to create a square. Press the square with an iron. Open the C block. The center will be where the two folds meet. Appliqué a heart to the center of the C block.

Mark the shape of the flower 1½ inches from the heart's top and bottom. Mark a flower shape 1½ inches from each side.

Appliqué a vine between flower markings so that a little of the vine overlaps the flower shape. Appliqué leaves to vines as shown. Appliqué a flower shape and center to each of the places indicated in the diagram. Mark hearts in each corner of the C block. Be sure the bottom of the heart points towards the center.

Sew an A strip to the top and bottom edge of the C block. Also, sew an A strip to each side of the C block. Then sew a white B strip to the top and bottom edge of the patchwork and to each side. Now sew an A strip to the top and bottom edge of the white B strip and to each edge.

Mark a border on the white B strip. Mark a flower shape on each corner, the center bottom, and the top B strip. The flowers should line up with the center heart and the top and bottom flowers on the C block. Mark a flower shape on each side of the B strip. Be sure the flower is lined up with the center heart and with side flowers on the C block. Trace a vine shape on each side of the flowers. See illustration for placement. Also trace leaves. Finally, fill in the hearts between the flowers as shown in the diagram.

Appliqué the flowers, vines, leaves, and hearts on the marked B strip.

Cut a back and a Fiberfil block for the whole quilt, using the front as a pattern. Put the back, Fiberfil block, and front together, lining the edges exactly. Baste them vertically and horizontally with contrasting thread.

Quilt the wall hanging by using outline quilting and going around each appliqué shape. Also outline the C block and the B strips. Remove basting and bind the wall hanging.

For hanging, sew brackets to each top back edge, and add a bracket in the center.

Hearts-and-Flowers Templates

Seam allowance: ¼ inch

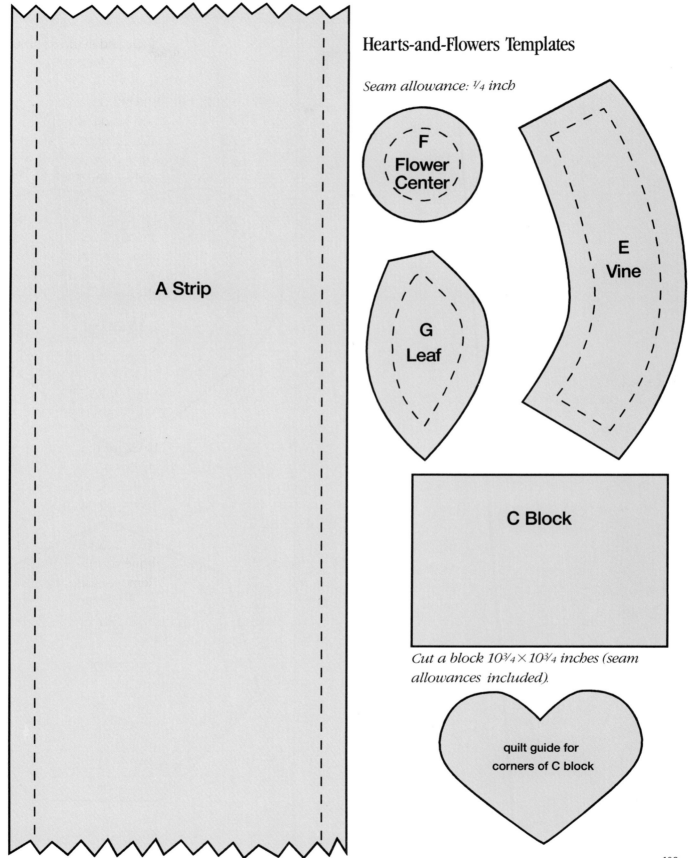

A Strip

F Flower Center

E Vine

G Leaf

C Block

Cut a block 10¾ × 10¾ inches (seam allowances included).

quilt guide for corners of C block

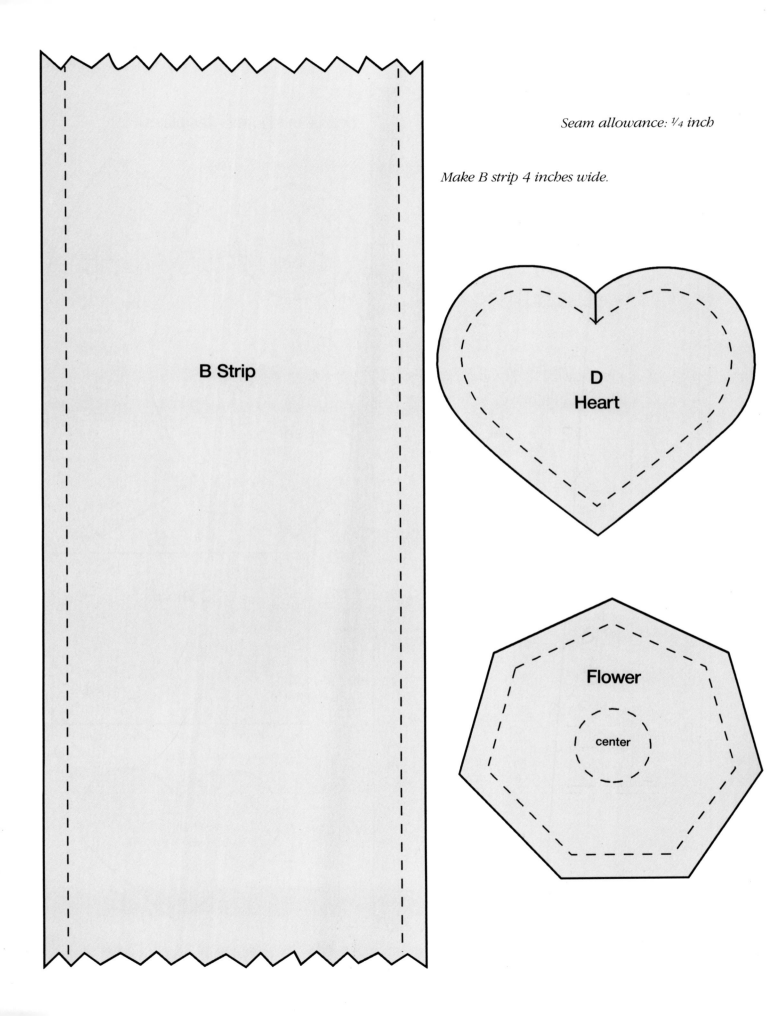

B Strip

Seam allowance: ¼ inch

Make B strip 4 inches wide.

D Heart

Flower

center

Quilt Assembly

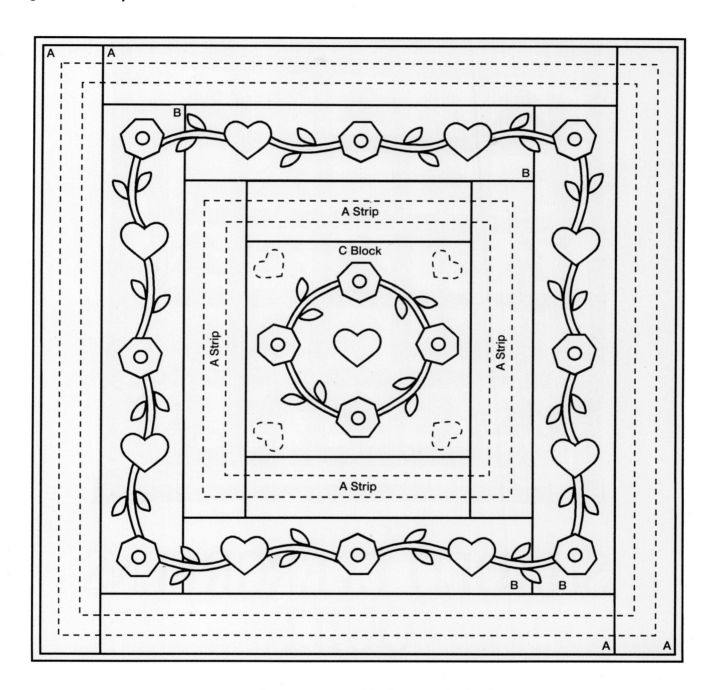

Corner hearts in center block are quilted only.

SHADED EVERGREENS QUILT

Supplies

½ yard of light green print for trees and border patchwork

½ yard of medium green print for trees and border patchwork

1 yard of dark green print for trees and border patchwork

3 yards of medium-dark fabric for G connecting lattice and border

¼ yard of rust or brown for tree trunks

2 yards of white fabric for border strip and C's and D's on trees

6 yards of fabric for quilt back

3½ yards of 60-inch-wide lightweight Fiberfil

10 yards of binding

quilting hoop

water-erasable quilt-marking pen

quilting needle

quilting thread

Directions

Finished size: 82 × 82 inches

Make twenty-five tree blocks—thirteen dark, six medium, and six light green, all with white or light background. See the assembly diagram.

Next, prepare the border strips, following the border assembly diagram.

With this preparation done, you're ready to assemble the quilt top. Follow the eleven-step diagrams for quilt top assembly.

Next, prepare the quilt back, consulting the general instructions in the Quilting Basics chapter. With a water-erasable quilt-marking pen and guide provided, mark the quilt for quilting. Put the back, Fiberfil, and quilt top together, and baste them vertically and horizontally, using a running stitch.

Using a quilting hoop, begin in the center of the quilt and quilt outward. When you complete your quilting, remove the basting thread.

Sew binding around the quilt's edges. Turn the binding to the back of the quilt, and sew the binding edge to the quilt by hand, making sure no stitches show on the front of the quilt.

Amounts given are for one block. Make twenty-five tree blocks—six light, six medium, and thirteen dark green.

Seam allowance: ¼ inch

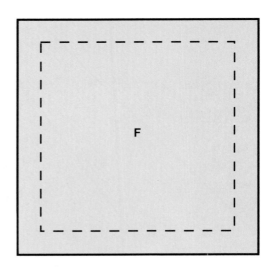

Cut one.

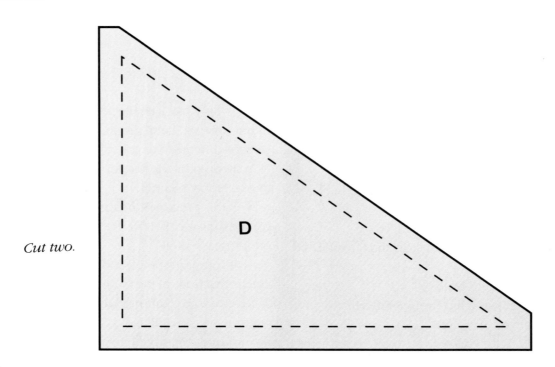

Cut two.

D

Cut one.

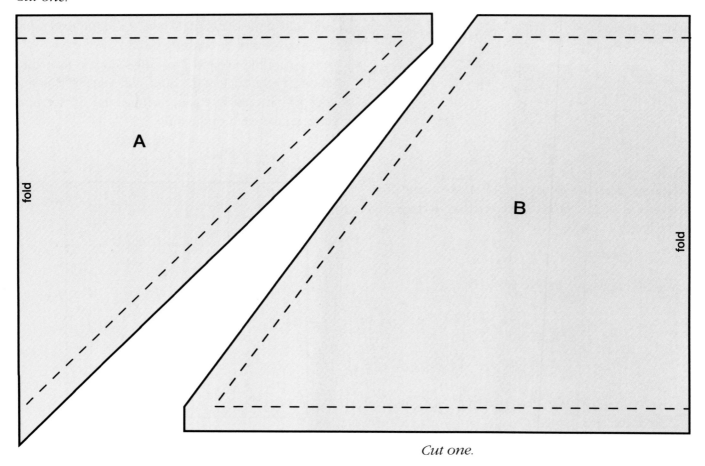

A

fold

B

fold

Cut one.

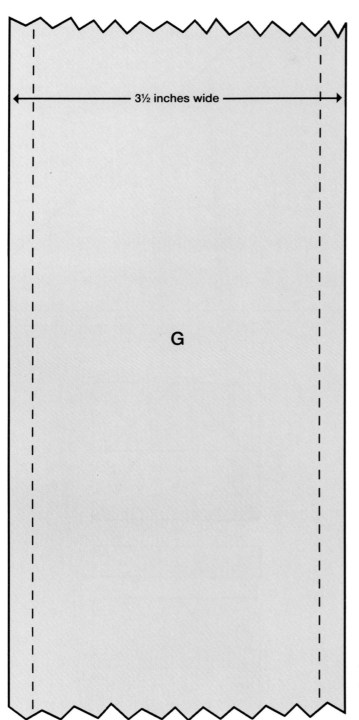

3½ inches wide

G

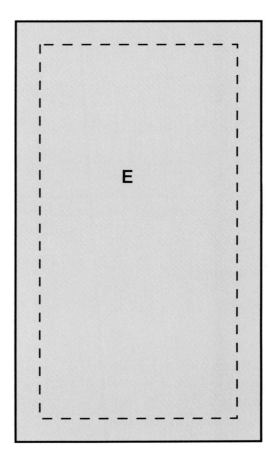

E

Cut two.

Make connecting lattice 3½ inches wide for blocks and borders.

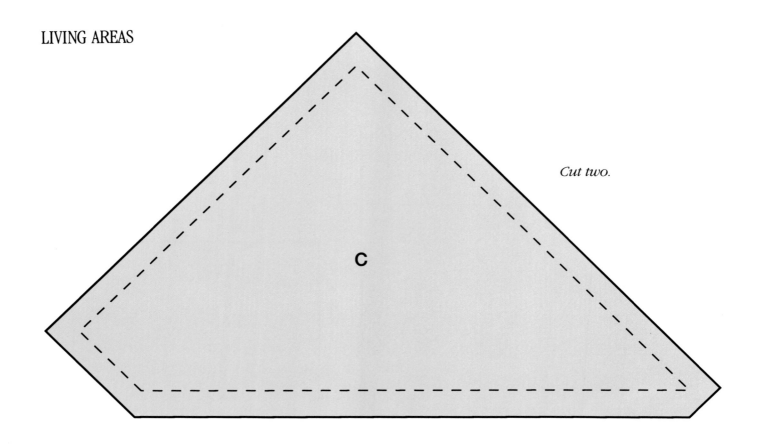

Cut two.

Block Assembly

1. Sew a C to each side of A.

2. Sew a D to each side of B.

3. Sew an A–C block to a D–B block.

4. Sew an E to each side of F.

5. Sew an E–F to the bottom edge.

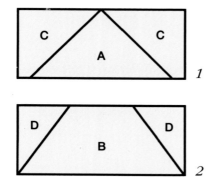

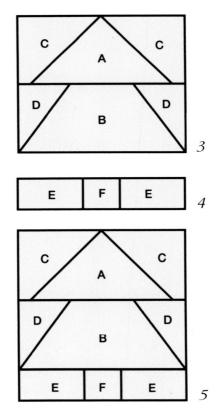

Border

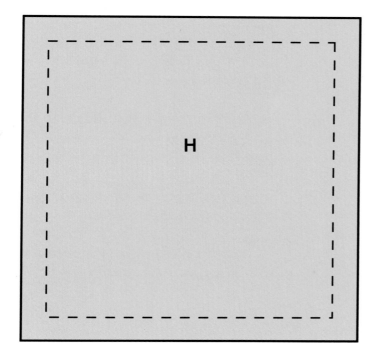

Cut four.

The amounts given are for the entire border of patchwork—all four corners.

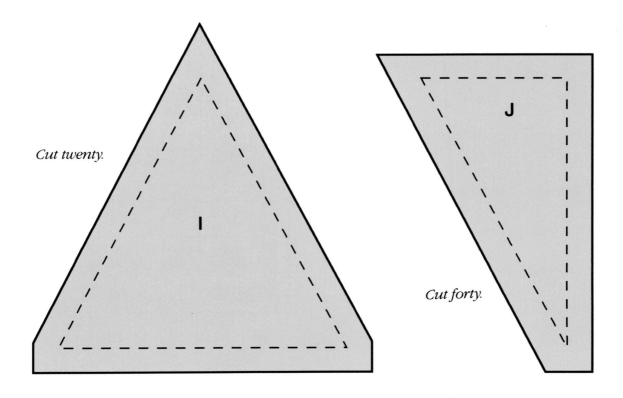

Cut twenty.

Cut forty.

Border Assembly

1. Sew a J to each side of I.

2. Sew five J–I blocks together as shown. Note color values; all J's are white. Make eight.

3. Sew an H to the top edge of four of the J–I chains as shown.

4. Cut out four G strips 3½ × 38½ inches.

5. Sew a J–I–H strip to each end of the two G strips. This completes the vertical border.

6. Sew a J–I strip to each end of the remaining two G strips. This completes the horizontal border.

6. Connect the strips using four lattice strips between the five tree strips and the remaining two across the top and bottom as shown.

7. Cut two strips the same length as the quilt top, using G as a guide for the width. Sew the strips to the quilt's sides as shown.

8. Attach the border. First, sew the horizontal strip (J–I–G) to the top and the bottom, then the vertical strip (J–I–H–G) to each side.

9. Sew a G strip to the top and bottom edge that's the same width as the quilt top.

10. Finish the top by sewing G strips to the sides that are the same length as the top.

Quilt Top Assembly

1. Cut twenty strips 10½ inches long, using G as a guide for width.

2. Sew a strip to the bottom edge of the tree block.

3. Sew a tree to the bottom edge as shown.

4. Sew a strip of five trees. Make five strips.

5. Use G as a guide for width. Cut six strips the same length as five tree strips.

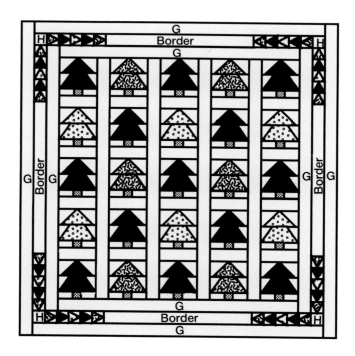

Quilting Guide

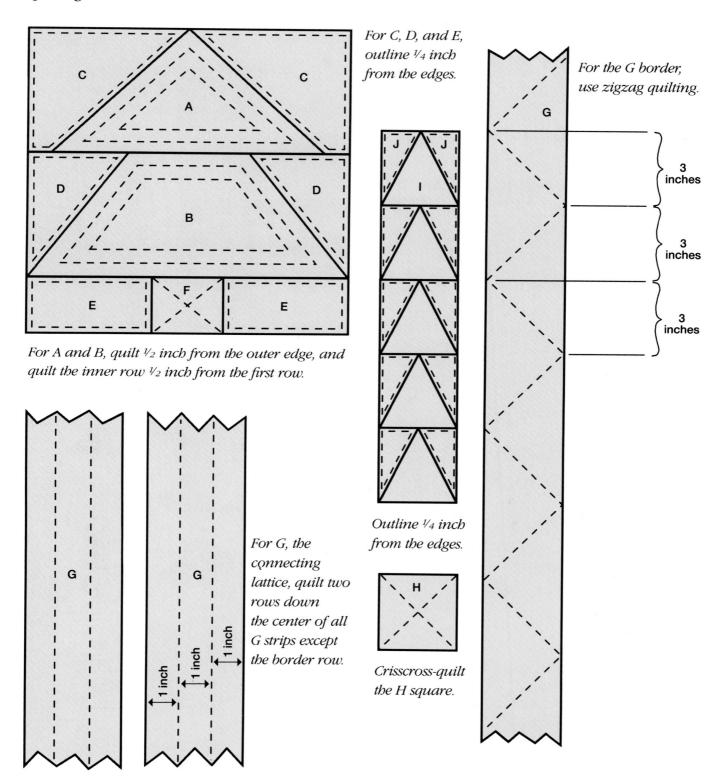

For C, D, and E, outline ¼ inch from the edges.

For the G border, use zigzag quilting.

3 inches

3 inches

3 inches

For A and B, quilt ½ inch from the outer edge, and quilt the inner row ½ inch from the first row.

Outline ¼ inch from the edges.

For G, the connecting lattice, quilt two rows down the center of all G strips except the border row.

Crisscross-quilt the H square.

HOLIDAYS

I *really love holidays! They break up the monotony of the every day and bring celebrations into our*
lives. Although some holidays are not as important as others in the way we celebrate them, any
holiday can be fun for creating decorations and making delectable food for friends and family.

The nine projects in this chapter can adorn your house and add to the spirit of various holidays.
Quilters may feel the need, as I do, to make their own decorations of uniquely quilted or stitched
fabrics for these times. You'll also need to reserve a place, such as a closet or cedar chest, in your house
for storing these adornments. I hope these projects become holiday favorites for your family, and that as
festive times approach, you'll look forward to bringing out the decoration(s) you have on hand.

Of course, Christmas is the most widely celebrated holiday in the world. Filling the house with tokens
of Christmas is always a joy. I began my own construction of the Christmas projects with a scrappy
quilt, a Nine-Patch in a Nine-Patch. *You'll have fun collecting lots of different prints in red and green*
from your favorite fabric stores. Often quilting stores make up ¼-yard pieces and sell them at a low
price. This quilt requires a variety of fabrics to give it the scrappy look.

The "I Love Christmas" wall hanging reflects how many people feel about the holiday. Evergreen
trees and hearts combine with patchwork to create this festive banner. Place mats and napkins add a
nice touch for a Christmas dinner.

The Christmas collection is completed with the Christmas Baskets *wall hanging. I have real affection*
for baskets and love almost every patchwork basket pattern I see. I have combined a basket pattern
with four traditional winter berries—holly, cranberry, pyracantha, and mistletoe. The border is also
adorned with small baskets filled with berries.

Valentine's Day is a wonderful time to celebrate love and romance. The fabric Valentine project,
"Tell Me, My Heart, If This Be Love" wall hanging combines appliqué, embroidery, and patchwork. This
heart could be a surprise gift for the one you love on that special day.

Whether or not you're Irish, it's fun to celebrate St. Patrick's Day. This is a time for soda bread, beef
stew, and leprechauns. You can hang the St. Patrick's Day Wreath *described in this chapter on your front*
door or in your dining room.

CHRISTMAS BASKETS
WALL HANGING

Supplies

1¼ yards of red fabric for B's, F's, handles, and V blocks on border and center

½ yard of white fabric for basket background blocks A, C, and D

⅛ yard of four different dark green print fabrics for leaves

½ yard of brown bias tape

½ yard of green bias tape

⅓ yard of red-and-white print fabric for E strip

1⅓ yard of white-and-red pin-dot fabric for the holly basket block light B's, light V border blocks, and X's and Y's on small basket blocks

scrap of white and green pin-dot fabric for mistletoe

scraps of four different red prints for berries on the pyracantha, cranberry, holly, and small basket

scrap of dark green for small basket handles

⅛ yard of cream-and-red print fabric for light B blocks on mistletoe basket

⅛ yard of second cream-and-red print fabric for light B blocks on cranberry basket

⅛ yard white-and-red check for light B's on holly basket block

¾ yard of green fabric for G's and V's on border

⅓ yard of another green print for V's on border

⅛ yard of red print for Z's on small basket

block of Fiberfil at least 42 × 42 inches

4⅔ yards of binding

quilting needle

quilting thread

Directions

Finished size: 41 × 41 inches

Make four patchwork baskets according to the finished basket diagram. Assemble the baskets following these steps.

1. Cut a bias strip 1¼ inches wide to use as a basket handle. This includes a ¼-inch seam allowance on each side and a ⅝-inch-wide handle. Make a handle at least 10 inches long. Appliqué the handle to the C pattern piece, following the pattern outline.

2. Sew light and dark B's together to form strips shown on the pattern. Note that the holly and pyracantha baskets use red and white light B's and that the cranberry and mistletoe baskets use cream and red light B's.

3. Sew the B–B strips together to form a triangle.

4. Sew the C–handle triangle to the B+B triangle to form a square block.

5. Sew a B to an A strip edge. Make two. See the diagram for the correct way to join edges.

6. Sew an A–B strip to the bottom and right side edge of the block.

7. Sew a D triangle to the lower right corner to complete the block.

Sew a G triangle to each corner of the basket blocks, making them into a square. The baskets will be sewn to the wall hanging on point.

See the diagrams for where to appliqué the berries—holly, cranberry, pyracantha, and mistletoe—to each basket.

Use brown bias tape for stems in the holly basket (3½ inches each for A and B) and the mistletoe basket (5½ inches for A and 6 inches for B). Use green bias tape for stems of the cranberry basket (3½ inches for A, 3½ inches for B, 4¼ inches for C, and 2½ inches for D) and the pyracantha basket (4 inches for A).

Assemble the wall hanging top, all except the border.

1. Sew an E strip to the right side of the holly basket block. Next, sew the mistletoe block to the right side of that E strip.

2. Measure and cut two E strips the same length as a basket block. Sew an E strip to each side of a dark red V block.

3. Now sew an E–V–E strip to the bottom edge of the patchwork.

4. Next, sew an E strip to the right side of the cranberry basket block. To that E strip's right side, sew the pyracantha basket block. Now sew a cranberry–E–pyracantha patchwork to the bottom edge of the E–V–E strip.

5. Last, sew an E strip to the top and bottom edge of the patchwork. Sew an E strip to each side of the patchwork.

Now, prepare the border by making eight small baskets. Then make eight V strips by sewing three rows of V's together following these steps for *each* V strip: Sew eleven V's together, alternating with light and medium green fabric. Make two rows like this. Then sew eleven V's together, alternating with red and white fabric. Make just one row. Sew these three rows together with the red and white V row in middle.

To make a border for the wall hanging, sew a V block strip to each side of a small basket. Make two. Sew the strips just formed to the top and bottom edges of the wall hanging.

Next, sew a V strip to the top and bottom edge of a small basket. Sew a small basket to the top and bottom ends of that strip. Make two. Now, sew these strips to each side of the wall hanging. This completes the border and the wall hanging's top.

Use the wall hanging top as a pattern to cut out a back and Fiberfil shape. Set the back, Fiberfil, and top together lined up exactly. Baste them vertically and horizontally with contrasting thread.

Quilt the wall hanging using outline quilting. Remove the basting and bind the wall hanging. Sew the three brackets to the back of the quilt's top edge—one on the end and one on each side.

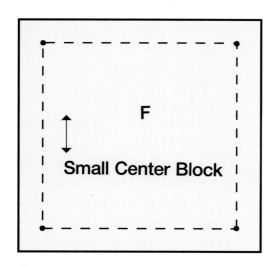

Cut one.

Make A strips 2½ × 6½ inches.
Make E strips 2½ inches wide.

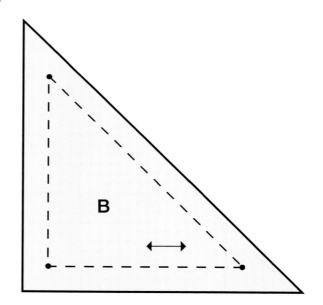

Seam allowance: ¼ inch, unless otherwise specified

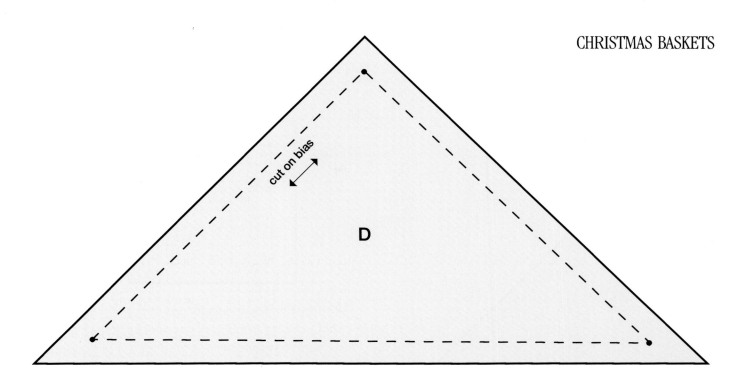

D

cut on bias

Minibasket Block for Border

Make eight baskets; amounts given are for one basket.

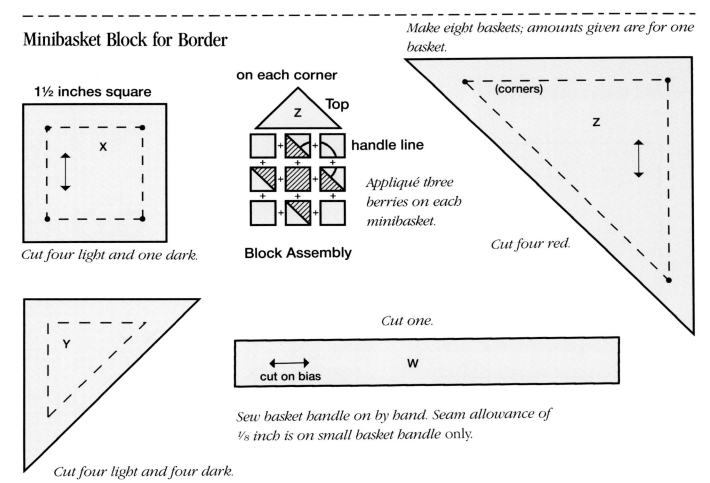

1½ inches square

X

Cut four light and one dark.

on each corner

Z

Top

handle line

Appliqué three berries on each minibasket.

Block Assembly

(corners)

Z

Cut four red.

Y

Cut four light and four dark.

Cut one.

W

cut on bias

*Sew basket handle on by hand. Seam allowance of
⅛ inch is on small basket handle only.*

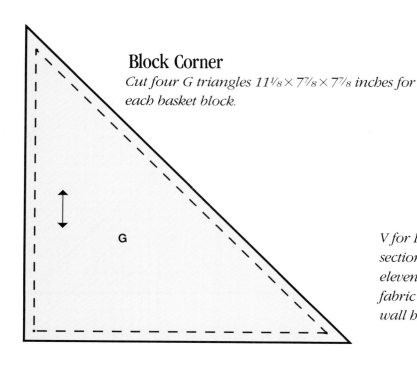

Block Corner

Cut four G triangles 11⅛ × 7⅞ × 7⅞ inches for each basket block.

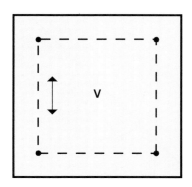

V for Border Blocks—eight sections; for each section, cut six white and red pin-dot, five red, eleven dark green fabric 1, and eleven dark green fabric 2. Also cut one V block for the center of the wall hanging.

Finished Basket Block

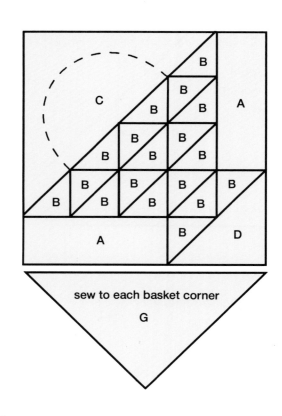

sew to each basket corner

G

Quilt Assembly

The four Christmas berry baskets include, clockwise from upper left: holly, mistletoe, cranberry, and pyracantha.

Berries and leaves have ⅛-inch seam allowances.

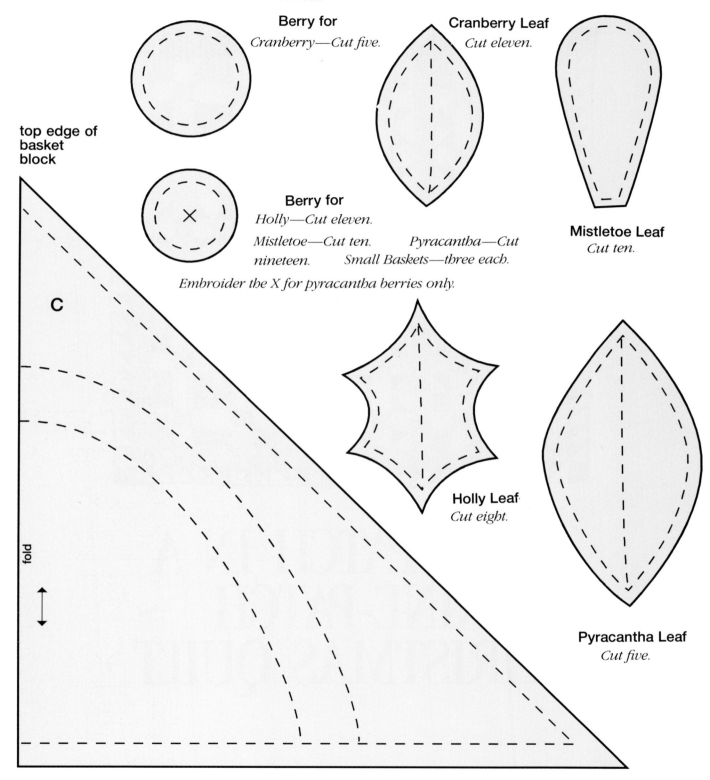

Berry for
Cranberry—Cut five.

Cranberry Leaf
Cut eleven.

top edge of basket block

Berry for

Holly—Cut eleven.

Mistletoe—Cut ten.   *Pyracantha—Cut*
nineteen.   *Small Baskets—three each.*

Embroider the X for pyracantha berries only.

Mistletoe Leaf
Cut ten.

C

fold

Holly Leaf
Cut eight.

Pyracantha Leaf
Cut five.

NINE-PATCH IN A NINE-PATCH CHRISTMAS QUILT

Supplies

2½ yards of white fabric for patchwork

1 yard of medium green for D strips

½ yard of pin-dot dark green fabric for border (dark C's)

¼ yard of red print fabric for border center

¾ yard of solid red fabric for A's (connecting), C's, and B's (border)

scraps of dark and medium green print fabrics for B's and C's

4½ yards of lightweight bonded Fiberfil

4¼ yards of green and red print fabric for backing

8¼ yards of binding

quilting needle

quilting thread

quilting hoop

Seam allowance: ¼ inch

Amounts given are for a single basic block.

Directions

Finished size: 72 × 72 inches

Make thirty-six basic blocks following the assembly diagram. Then create jumbo blocks, following the diagram for jumbo block assembly. Sew these jumbo blocks and D strips into rows.

Sew the rows together separated by A–1 joiner strips. Also sew an A–1 joiner strip to the top and bottom of the quilt top. Sew an A–2 joiner strip to each side of the quilt top.

Make border strips for the top and bottom edges, following the diagram. Make two side border strips, and sew them to each side of the quilt top. Sew the top border strip to the top edge of the quilt top and the bottom border strip to the bottom edge of the quilt top. The quilt top is now completed.

Baste the quilt top, Fiberfil, and back together (see Quilting Basics). Quilt with outline quilting on the light-colored blocks. Bind the quilt, and remove the basting.

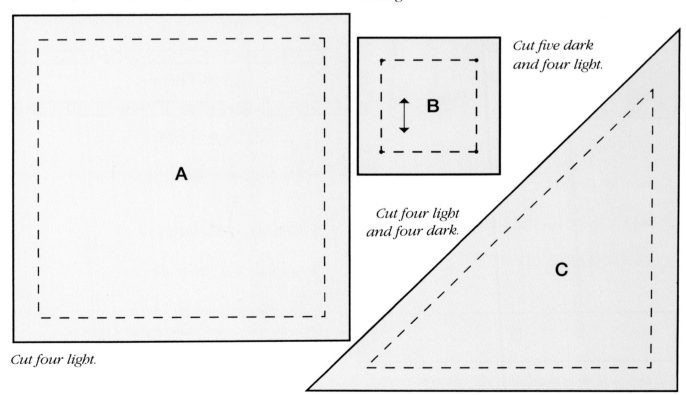

A

Cut four light.

B

Cut four light and four dark.

Cut five dark and four light.

C

Cut four light and four dark.

Basic Block Assembly

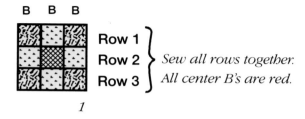

B B B

Row 1
Row 2   } *Sew all rows together.*
Row 3   } *All center B's are red.*

1

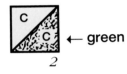

C
C ← **green**

2

Some of these C's will be white, and some red, according to your taste.

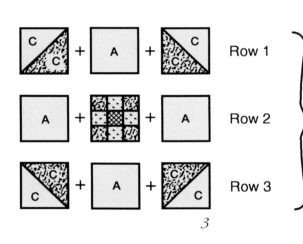

C / C + A + C / C   Row 1

A + (checkered) + A   Row 2

C / C + A + C / C   Row 3

3

1. *Sew nine B's together like this.*

2. *Sew a C to a C like this. Make four.*

3. *Assemble the basic block.*

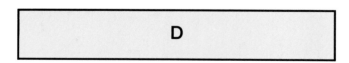

D

Cut twenty-four D strips 3½ × 18½ inches.

Jumbo Block Assembly

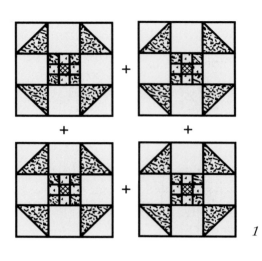

+
+   +
+

1

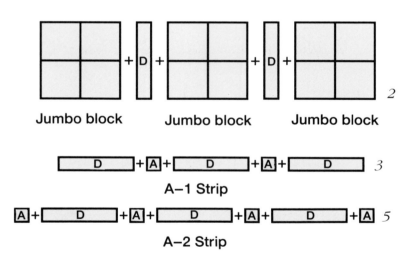

Jumbo block +D+ **Jumbo block** +D+ **Jumbo block**

2

D +A+ D +A+ D   *3*

A–1 Strip

A+ D +A+ D +A+ D +A   *5*

A–2 Strip

1. *Sew four basic blocks together to form a jumbo block.*

2. *Make three rows like this.*

3. *Sew four A–1 joiner strips.*

4. *Sew the rows together with A–1 joiner strips in between rows and on the top and bottom of the quilt.*

5. *Sew two A–2 joiner strips, and sew them to each side of the quilt top. This completes the top.*

Border Detail

Top Border Strip

A
Dark  A
Dark

Bottom Border Strip

Side Border Strips

"I LOVE CHRISTMAS"

Supplies

⅓ yard of dark red for J strips and back

¼ yard of white for H, I, G, B, D, and F

scraps of green and red fabric for E blocks, hearts, and trees

scrap of brown fabric for tree trunk

square of lightweight Fiberfil 13 × 17 inches

package of red single-fold bias tape for binding

skein of red embroidery thread

skein of dark green embroidery thread

water-erasable marking pen

quilting needle

quilting thread

brackets for hanging

Directions

Finished size: 13 × 17 inches

Prepare the sign's front first. Trace the H and I block outlines on white fabric. Centered inside the I block, trace "*I LOVE*." Centered inside the H block, trace "*CHRISTMAS*." Use a chain stitch with three strands of embroidery thread to embroider "*I*" and "*CHRISTMAS*" in dark green and "*LOVE*" in red. Now cut out the H and I blocks.

Sew a row of E blocks—two red and two green in alternating colors. Make two rows. Sew the rows together so that reds and greens alternate. Make two of these eight-block units. See patchwork assembly step 1. Now sew three E's with alternating colors—red–green–red. Then sew another three E's together—green–red–green. Sew strips together, keeping alternating colors. Make two units like this; see patchwork assembly step 2.

Next, assemble the trees. Sew a white B to each side of the green A (see tree patchwork assembly step 1). Sew a white D to each side of the dark green C (see step 2). Sew a white F to each side of the brown E (see step 3). Sew these three newly created rows together (see step 4). Make two trees.

Appliqué the top heart and bottom heart to the G block.

To assemble the front of the wall hanging, sew eight E strips to each side of the I block to form a rectangular strip. Sew a J strip to the top and bottom edge of the strip just formed. Sew a J strip to each side of the appliquéd hearts block (G).

Then sew a tree block to each side of the G–J strip. Sew six E strips to each side of the H block. Sew a J to the top and bottom of the H–E strip, and sew the strips together as shown in finished diagram. Finally, sew a J strip to each side of the wall hanging to complete the front.

Use the wall hanging front as a pattern to cut out a back and a Fiberfil shape. Line up the back, Fiberfil, and front, matching the edges exactly, and baste the three layers together.

Quilt the wall hanging, using outline quilting on the light blocks G, H, and I, and the backgrounds of tree blocks. Quilt around the red E blocks. Remove the basting. Bind the edges of the wall hanging. Sew the hanging brackets to the top back of the wall hanging—one on the center, and one on each corner.

Use E blocks also for the top and bottom next to the word strips: cut fourteen red and fourteen green.

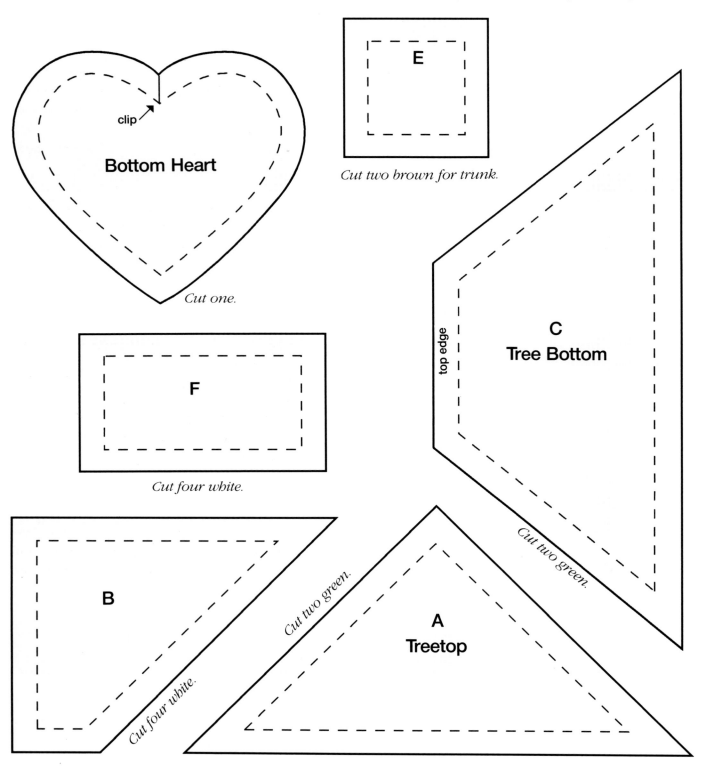

Bottom Heart

clip

Cut one.

E

Cut two brown for trunk.

F

Cut four white.

C
Tree Bottom

top edge

Cut two green.

B

Cut four white.

Cut two green.

A
Treetop

Top Heart

Cut one.

D

Cut four white.

Cut one H strip 2½×9½ inches.

Cut one I strip 2½×7½ inches.

Make G strip 3½×5½ inches.

Patchwork Assembly

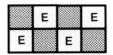

1. Make two like this; alternate red and green blocks.

2. Make two like this; alternate red and green blocks.

Tree Patchwork Assembly

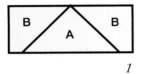

1

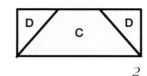

2

3

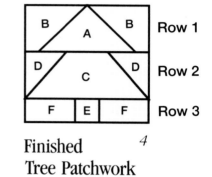

Row 1

Row 2

Row 3

4

Finished
Tree Patchwork

Complete Quilt Assembly

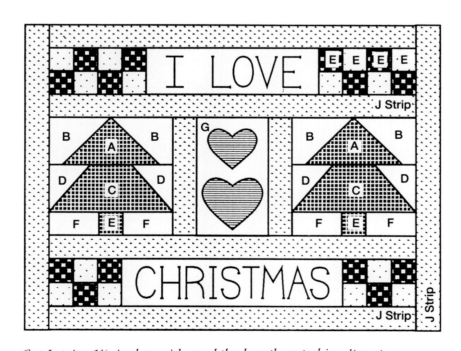

Cut J strips 1½ inches wide and the length noted in directions.

ST. PATRICK'S DAY WREATH

Supplies

12-inch-diameter grape vine wreath
scraps of orange fabric for hearts
scraps of light green fabric for shamrocks
scraps of dark green fabric for shamrocks
scrap of muslin for banner
green thread
orange thread
sprigs of dusty miller, heather, and green mimex
   (available at floral supply stores)
2 yards of ⅝-inch-wide light green ribbon
2 yards of ⅝-inch-wide dark green ribbon
green thread
orange thread
quilting needles, quilting thread
glue gun

Directions

Finished size: 12 inches round

Make two light green shamrocks and two dark green shamrocks following the diagram steps. Make three orange hearts, and make the "IRELAND" banner.

Quilt around the inner edge of the shamrocks and hearts with two rows of quilting. Thread both the light and the dark green ribbons in and out of the grape vine wreath, beginning at the bottom and ending with the bottom. Lengths of ribbon should remain hanging down. Trim the ribbon ends with a cut groove (see illustration).

With a glue gun, glue the "IRELAND" banner over the center bottom edge of the wreath. Glue an orange heart to the wreath center top. Then glue a light green shamrock on each side of the orange heart about 1½ inches from the heart. About 1 inch from the light green shamrock, glue an orange heart to each side of the wreath. Finally, glue a green shamrock about 1½ inches down from the orange heart.

Fill in the wreath by gluing strips of dusty miller, heather, and green mimex. For hanging, tie a small length of ribbon to form a circle to the top of the wreath.

Machine-Appliqué for Shamrocks, Ireland Banner, and Hearts

Ribbon Ends

cut like this

No seam allowances

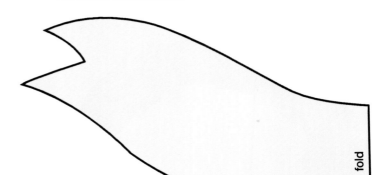

Banner for Words

Cut two—one back and one front.

1. *Trace the shamrock shape on the fabric to be used for shamrock.*

2. *Cut a block of bonded Fiberfil and a back of fabric.*

3. *Baste the three layers together.*

4. *Machine-stitch (satin stitch) around the shamrock shape through the three layers.*

5. *With sharp scissors, trim away the excess fabric from the shape as close to the satin stitch as possible. Be careful not to cut into the machine stitching.*

6. *Remove basting.*

7. *For the Ireland banner, trace the shape and the word "IRELAND." Embroider the word first, then machine-stitch around the edge. Complete, following steps 5 and 6 above.*

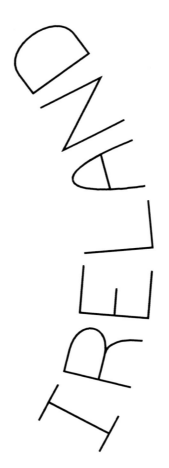

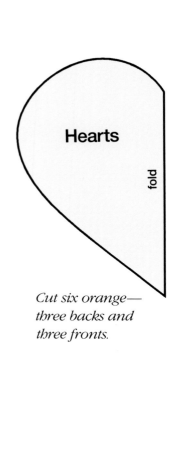

Hearts

fold

Cut six orange— three backs and three fronts.

"TELL ME, MY HEART, IF THIS BE LOVE" WALL HANGING

Supplies

⅓ yard of cream and red light fabric for C center block

⅛ yard of white fabric for A blocks

½ yard of dark red print for B outer strips and back

scraps of fabric, medium blue for birds, light blue for birds' wings, light green for leaves, medium red for small heart, and dark red for large heart

⅓ yard of ⅛-inch-wide green braid for vine

skein of dark red embroidery thread for words

skein of dark blue embroidery thread for birds' eyes

block of bonded Fiberfil at least 15 × 20 inches

2 yards of binding

2 lightweight brackets for hanging

quilting needles, quilting thread

Directions

Finished size: 14 × 18 inches

Trace the template for vines, leaves, heart, and birds, centered on the cream and red center C block. Mark the birds' eyes for embroidery. Appliqué the vines, leaves, heart, and birds, following the lines of the diagrams below. Embroider birds' eyes with a satin stitch.

Noting the finished diagram, appliqué the four smaller hearts on the front of the wall hanging. Now, sew an A to the top and bottom of the C block. Next, sew a B strip to the top and bottom of the patchwork and to each side.

Trace the words *"TELL ME, MY HEART,"* to the top A, and trace *"IF THIS BE LOVE"* to the bottom A. Embroider the words with a chain stitch. Trace the quilting design to the wall hanging front. See the quilting diagram and use the pattern provided.

Use the wall hanging as a pattern to cut out a back and a Fiberfil shape the same size. Place the back, Fiberfil, and top together, and baste them vertically and horizontally.

Quilt the wall hanging. Bind the edges, and remove the basting. Sew the brackets for hanging to each side of the top back.

Quilting Guide

Quilt three hearts between each appliquéd heart for twelve appliquéd hearts all together.

Quilt two rows on B; quilt around the main block and around the heart, vine, birds, and leaves.

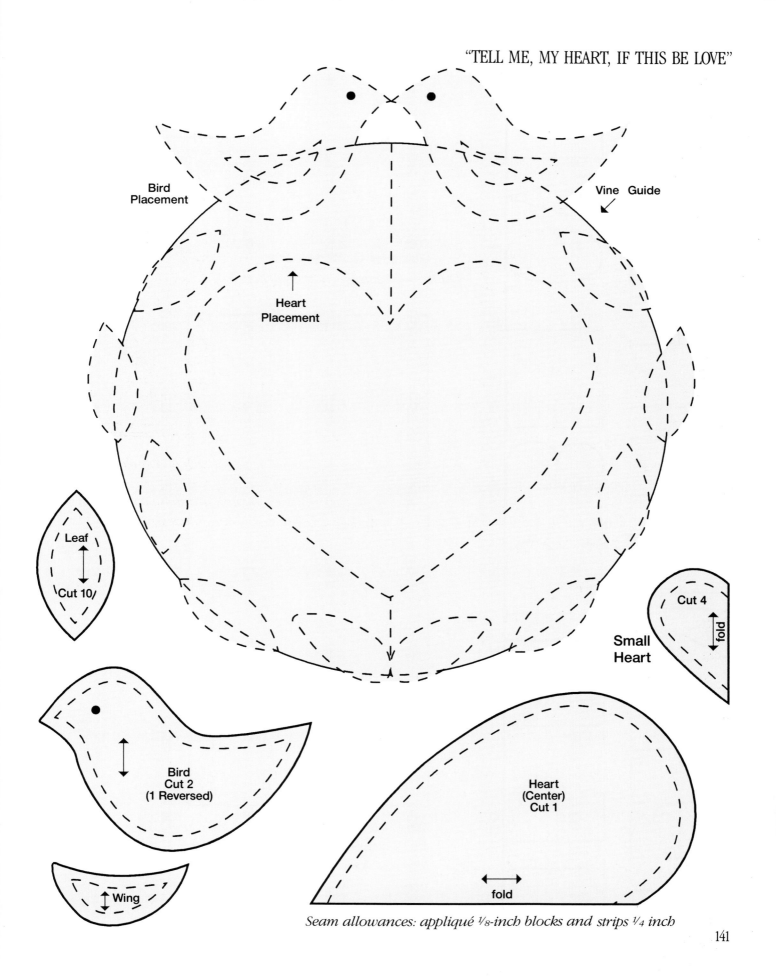

Bird Placement

Vine Guide

Heart Placement

Leaf
Cut 10

Small Heart

Cut 4

fold

Bird
Cut 2
(1 Reversed)

Heart
(Center)
Cut 1

fold

Wing

Seam allowances: appliqué ⅛-inch blocks and strips ¼ inch

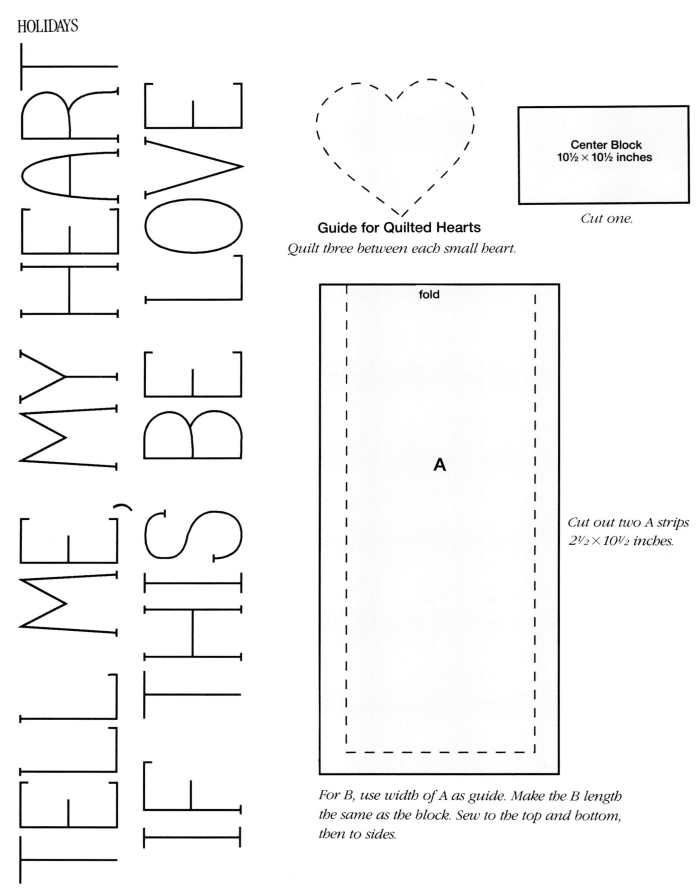

TELL ME, MY HEART
IF THIS BE LOVE

Guide for Quilted Hearts

Quilt three between each small heart.

Center Block
10½ × 10½ inches

Cut one.

fold

A

Cut out two A strips
2½ × 10½ inches.

*For B, use width of A as guide. Make the B length
the same as the block. Sew to the top and bottom,
then to sides.*

METRIC EQUIVALENCY CHART

MM—MILLIMETRES   CM—CENTIMETRES

INCHES TO MILLIMETRES AND CENTIMETRES

INCHES	MM	CM	INCHES	CM	INCHES	CM
⅛	3	0.3	9	22.9	30	76.2
¼	6	0.6	10	25.4	31	78.7
⅜	10	1.0	11	27.9	32	81.3
½	13	1.3	12	30.5	33	83.8
⅝	16	1.6	13	33.0	34	86.4
¾	19	1.9	14	35.6	35	88.9
⅞	22	2.2	15	38.1	36	91.4
1	25	2.5	16	40.6	37	94.0
1¼	32	3.2	17	43.2	38	96.5
1½	38	3.8	18	45.7	39	99.1
1¾	44	4.4	19	48.3	40	101.6
2	51	5.1	20	50.8	41	104.1
2½	64	6.4	21	53.3	42	106.7
3	76	7.6	22	55.9	43	109.2
3½	89	8.9	23	58.4	44	111.8
4	102	10.2	24	61.0	45	114.3
4½	114	11.4	25	63.5	46	116.8
5	127	12.7	26	66.0	47	119.4
6	152	15.2	27	68.6	48	121.9
7	178	17.8	28	71.1	49	124.5
8	203	20.3	29	73.7	50	127.0

YARDS TO METRES

YARDS	METRES	YARDS	METRES	YARDS	METRES	YARDS	METRES	YARDS	METRES
⅛	0.11	2⅛	1.94	4⅛	3.77	6⅛	5.60	8⅛	7.43
¼	0.23	2¼	2.06	4¼	3.89	6¼	5.72	8¼	7.54
⅜	0.34	2⅜	2.17	4⅜	4.00	6⅜	5.83	8⅜	7.66
½	0.46	2½	2.29	4½	4.11	6½	5.94	8½	7.77
⅝	0.57	2⅝	2.40	4⅝	4.23	6⅝	6.06	8⅝	7.89
¾	0.69	2¾	2.51	4¾	4.34	6¾	6.17	8¾	8.00
⅞	0.80	2⅞	2.63	4⅞	4.46	6⅞	6.29	8⅞	8.12
1	0.91	3	2.74	5	4.57	7	6.40	9	8.23
1⅛	1.03	3⅛	2.86	5⅛	4.69	7⅛	6.52	9⅛	8.34
1¼	1.14	3¼	2.97	5¼	4.80	7¼	6.63	9¼	8.46
1⅜	1.26	3⅜	3.09	5⅜	4.91	7⅜	6.74	9⅜	8.57
1½	1.37	3½	3.20	5½	5.03	7½	6.86	9½	8.69
1⅝	1.49	3⅝	3.31	5⅝	5.14	7⅝	6.97	9⅝	8.80
1¾	1.60	3¾	3.43	5¾	5.26	7¾	7.09	9¾	8.92
1⅞	1.71	3⅞	3.54	5⅞	5.37	7⅞	7.20	9⅞	9.03
2	1.83	4	3.66	6	5.49	8	7.32	10	9.14

METRIC CONVERSION RULER

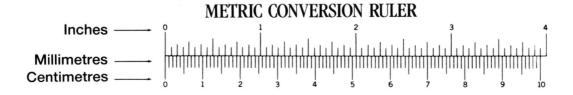

Inches ⟶

Millimetres ⟶

Centimetres ⟶

143

INDEX